W9-AWD-147

POWERFUL WORDS

POWERFUL WORDS

MORE THAN 200 YEARS OF EXTRAORDINARY WRITING BY AFRICAN AMERICANS

WADE HUDSON

Illustrated by **Sean Qualls**

Foreword by **Marian Wright Edelman**

SCHOLASTIC NONFICTION

To my wife and life partner,
Cheryl Willis Hudson,
my daughter Katura, and
my son Stephan for their love,
support and encouragement
—W.H.

Copyright © 2004 by Wade Hudson
Foreward copyright © 2004 by Marion Wright Edelman
All rights reserved. Published by Scholastic Inc.

SCHOLASTIC, SCHOLASTIC NONFICTION, and associated logos are
trademarks and/or registered trademarks of Scholastic Inc.

Text credits appear on p. 178.

Library of Congress Cataloging-in-Publication Data

Hudson, Wade. ★ Powerful words : more than 200 years of extraordinary writing by
African Americans / by Wade Hudson. ★   p.   cm. ★ Summary: A collection of speeches
and writings by African Americans, with commentary about the time period in which each
person lived, information about the speaker/writer, and public response to the words. ★
Includes bibliographical reference and index. ★ 1. African Americans—History—
Sources—Juvenile literature. 2. African Americans—Quotations—Juvenile literature.
3. African Americans—Biography—Juvenile literature. 4. Speeches, addresses, etc.,
American—African American authors—Juvenile literature. [1. African Americans—
History—Sources. 2. African Americans—Quotations. 3. Quotations. 4. African
Americans. 5. Speeches, addresses, etc.] I. Title. ★ E184.6.H83   2004 ★
081′.089′96073—dc21 2003042792 ★ ISBN 0-439-40969-1

10 9 8 7 6 5 4 3 2   04 05 06 07 08

Printed in the U.S.A.   24
First printing, February 2004

The text type was set in Mrs. Eaves and Rockwell.
Art direction by Nancy Sabato ★ Book design by Matt Bouloutian

CONTENTS

FOREWORD

Powerful Words is a wonderful collection of some of the most
important ideas black people have shared about our lives in the
United States. From Sojourner Truth to W.E.B. DuBois,
from Mary McLeod Bethune to Dr. Martin Luther King, Jr.,
from speeches and essays to stories and song lyrics, and from
the eighteenth century to the edge of the twenty-first, every
selection in this book tells us something important about the
world its author lived in—and in many cases, how she or he
tried to change it. African Americans have always had many
dreams and hopes about how to make America a better place
for black people and all Americans. There have been times in
American history when it was illegal for many blacks to learn to
read and write. When I was a girl, many black children were
still not allowed to attend school with white children. But even
in those difficult times and places, black people have always
found ways of putting our dreams into words.

 The words in this book are *by* African Americans, but they
are *for* all readers. I hope this book will introduce many of you
to authors you may not have known about and that their
thoughts will lead you to think about some new questions and
ideas. I especially hope they will inspire you to think about the
powerful words inside of *you.*

—MARIAN WRIGHT EDELMAN
President, Children's Defense Fund

Words can change things

INTRODUCTION

IN 1619 A DUTCH FRIGATE LANDED
AT JAMESTOWN, VIRGINIA. TWENTY
AFRICANS, THE FIRST TO BE
BROUGHT TO AMERICA AND SOLD,
WERE PART OF ITS CARGO. THE SALE
OF THESE AFRICANS IS GENERALLY
CONSIDERED TO BE THE BEGINNING
OF SLAVERY IN COLONIAL AMERICA.

But slavery as a system had not yet been firmly established in the new land. Some of these first Africans, and others who followed them, were able to buy their freedom after having earned enough money to do so. Others worked alongside whites who toiled as indentured servants.

During the early years, indentured servitude was the primary labor source in colonial America. But by 1700 it had been replaced by slavery. For the master, slavery had a marked advantage over servitude. The slave's service was for life. Indentured servants worked for a specified period of time, usually four to seven years. At the end of the servant's period, the master had to give him his freedom, a small sum of money, and a plot of land. With slavery, however, there were no such obligations. The slave was the property of his master. His offspring also became the property of the master.

The system of slavery was not instituted overnight. Gradually, law by law, practice by practice, colony by colony, and slave by slave, it grew. The great demand in Europe for tobacco, indigo, and rice grown in America fed the need for more slaves and helped to fertilize the growth of the slave trade.

When the Revolutionary War against the British began in 1775, nearly a half million African Americans were being held in slavery. The call for American freedom and independence was heard in every colony. Many of those who believed slavery was an unjust system felt that call applied to slavery as well. African Americans, free and enslaved, fought in the war that would win the colonies their independence. But it was soon made clear by the Founding Fathers that slavery would not be a part of this newly won freedom. It was "too valuable" to the American economy, particularly in the South.

Slavery continued to grow in America. Every year, thousands of captured Africans were added to the slave population. Though the end of slavery seemed far away, those who fought for its end continued to raise their voices in protest. Some, such as Benjamin Banneker, used the ideals expressed by the Founding Fathers to support their call for the freedom of African-American slaves. Banneker wrote a letter to Thomas Jefferson, author of the Declaration of Independence, who was then secretary of state in George Washington's cabinet. That letter is the first selection in *Powerful Words*.

As slavery continued to grow, so did the voices of protest against it. Developing during this time, too, was a growing African-American consciousness that was giving rise to African-American institutions, organizations, and identity. Richard Allen, founder of one of the earliest African-American churches, and John Russwurm and Samuel B.

Cornish, who together published the first African-American owned newspaper, are representative of this period. Antislavery crusaders such as David Walker, Frederick Douglass, Sojourner Truth, and Frances Ellen Watkins Harper are included. So is Dred Scott, whose petition for freedom led to one of the most infamous decisions of the United States Supreme Court.

The post—Civil War period features a selection by Blanche K. Bruce, the first African American to serve a full six-year term in the United States Senate. There is a speech by the genteel but powerful Mary Church Terrell, and an excerpt from *A Red Record*, written by Ida B. Wells Barnett, who launched an intense campaign to put an end to the lynching of African Americans.

As a new century loomed, African Americans were engaged in a great debate about the best way to achieve equality and justice. One philosophy was headed by Booker T. Washington, the other by W.E.B. DuBois. The views of both are a part of this collection.

Selections from the early 1900s include James Weldon and J. Rosamond Johnson's anthem "Lift Ev'ry Voice and Sing," and an article by herculean educator Mary McLeod Bethune. The post—World War I years include a speech by the militant Marcus Garvey and the Harlem Renaissance writings of Langston Hughes and Zora Neale Hurston. The monumental gospel song "Precious Lord, Take My Hand," by Thomas Dorsey, the "Father of Gospel Music," has a deserved place here, too.

When Richard Wright's novel about urban ghetto life, *Native Son,* was released in 1940, it shook the country. No other book had been as realistic and as brutally honest about the African-American experience. An excerpt from this powerful novel appears in this collection.

Also in *Powerful Words* is a speech by the multitalented and politically aware Paul Robeson and a poem by the scientist-inventor George Washington Carver.

The modern civil rights movement is generally considered to have begun in 1954 with the *Brown* v. *Board of Education of Topeka, Kansas,* Supreme Court decision that ended legalized segregation. An excerpt from the brief prepared by Thurgood Marshall and the National Association for the Advancement of Colored People legal team as well as other selections from Rosa Parks, Dr. Martin Luther King, Jr., and Malcolm X help to capture the tone, flavor, and importance of this period.

Selections representing the move toward militancy, political successes of the 1970s and 1980s, and leading voices for new causes are a part of *Powerful Words,* too.

This book covers more than two hundred years of African-American and American history. Through this collection, one can get a good glimpse of the African-American odyssey in America: the struggle against slavery, discrimination, and racism; the shaping of a national African-American community while an American nation is developing simultaneously; and the many contributions African Americans have made to help this nation develop.

Words can be powerful. Words can stir and motivate. Words can illuminate. Words can open the door to new and better ways of understanding. Words can change things. The African-American legacy is a rich one indeed. Read *Powerful Words* and you will understand why.

Wade Hudson
East Orange, New Jersey
July 2003

From a Letter to Thomas Jefferson ★ AUGUST 19, 1791

BENJAMIN BANNEKER

1731–1806

The Declaration of Independence had been issued. America had won its freedom from England. The Constitution of the United States had been drawn up and ratified. George Washington had been elected the first president. A young America was moving quickly to establish itself as a secure democratic republic.

African Americans, however, were not a part of this new burst of freedom. The number of slaves was growing at an alarming rate. Laws that discriminated against free African Americans were being implemented regularly. Many African Americans had fought for the country's independence, but it was clear they would not be able to enjoy that freedom.

A disillusioned Benjamin Banneker was moved to write a letter to Thomas Jefferson, who was secretary of state at the time. Banneker hoped to appeal to the love of freedom expressed by Jefferson in the Declaration of Independence and other documents.

**S**ir:——

I am fully sensible of the greatness of that freedom, which I take with you on the present occasion, a liberty which seemed to me scarcely allowable, when I reflected on that distinguished and dignified station in which you stand, and the almost general prejudice and prepossession which is so prevalent in the world against those of my complexion.

I suppose it is a truth too well attested to you, to need a proof here, that we are a race of beings who have long laboured under the abuse and censure of the world, that we have long been considered rather as brutish than human, and scarcely capable of mental endowments.

Sir, I hope I may safely admit, in consequence of the report which hath reached me, that you are a man far less inflexible in sentiments of this nature than many others, that you are measurably friendly and well disposed towards us, and that you are willing and ready to lend your aid and assistance to our relief, from those many distresses and numerous calamities, to which we are reduced.

Now, sir, if this is founded in truth, I apprehend you will readily embrace every opportunity to eradicate that train of absurd and false ideas and opinions, which so generally prevail with respect to us, and that your sentiments are concurrent with mine, which are that one universal Father

"THE COLOR OF THE SKIN IS IN NO WAY CONNECTED WITH STRENGTH OF THE MIND OR INTELLECTUAL POWERS."
—Benjamin Banneker

hath given Being to us all, and that he hath not only made us all of one flesh, but that he hath also without partiality afforded us all the same sensations, and endued us all with the same faculties, and that however variable we may be in society or religion, however diversified in situation or colour, we are all of the same family, and stand in the same relation to him ⋆

THE AUTHOR

Benjamin Banneker was an astronomer, surveyor, inventor, and publisher of several almanacs. He built a working clock with parts he made by hand. It is believed to be one of the first handmade clocks constructed in America.

Banneker was the first African American to receive a presidential appointment when George Washington named him to the commission that laid out the city of Washington, D.C. Banneker and Major Andrew Ellicott were chosen to assist Pierre Charles L'Enfant. President Washington dismissed L'Enfant following a disagreement, so the final calculations were left to Ellicott and Banneker. Considered one of the most brilliant minds of his time, Banneker died in 1806.

THE RESPONSE

Thomas Jefferson received Banneker's letter at his office in Philadelphia, Pennsylvania. The future president responded with a courteous letter of his own. In it he wrote that "he wishes to see a good system commenced for raising the condition" of enslaved African Americans. He forwarded a copy of Banneker's almanac, which Banneker had included with his letter, to a member of the Philanthropic Society and secretary of the Academy of Sciences at Paris. "I consider it as a document which your whole colour have a right for their justification against the doubts to which have been entertained of them," Jefferson wrote about the almanac. But the great American leader was not moved to take any action to end slavery.

From *The Life Experience and Gospel Labors
of the Right Rev. Richard Allen* ★ 1786

RICHARD ALLEN

1760–1831

When the first census was conducted in 1790, there were more than 750,000 African Americans in the United States. Of that total, 59,557 were free. Most free African Americans lived in the North or in large cities in the South.

Known as "free people of color," these African Americans faced discrimination daily. They were excluded from white society in almost every possible way. So they formed their own organizations, churches, and institutions. In doing so, they gave shape and form to black America. They were the Founding Fathers of black America.

Many consider Richard Allen the "Father of the Black Church" as well as the first American black leader. In his autobiography, he describes the incident that fertilized the growth of the black church movement in America.

**A**number of us usually attended St. George's Church in Fourth street [Philadelphia]; and when the coloured people began to get numerous in attending the church, they moved us from the seats we usually sat on, and placed us around the wall, and on Sabbath morning we went to church and the sexton stood at the door, and told us to go to the gallery. He told us to go, and we would see where to sit. We expected to take the seats over the ones we formerly occupied below, not knowing any better. We took those seats. Meeting had begun, and they were nearly done singing, and just as we got to the seats, the elder said, "Let us pray." We had not been long upon our knees before I heard considerable scuffling and low talking. I raised my head and saw one of the trustees, Mr. H—— M——, having hold of the Rev. Absalom Jones, pulling him up off his knees, and saying, "You must get up—you must not kneel here." Mr. Jones replied, "Wait until prayer is over." Mr. H—— M—— said "No, you must get up now, or I will call for aid and I will force you away." Mr. Jones said, "Wait until prayer is over, and I will get up and trouble you no more." With that he beckoned to one of the other trustees, Mr. L—— S—— to come to his assistance. He came, and went to William White to pull him up. By this time prayer was over, and we all went

"THE ONLY PLACE BLACKS FELT THEY COULD MAINTAIN AN ELEMENT OF SELF-EXPRESSION WAS THE CHURCH."
—Richard Allen

out of the church in a body, and they were no more plagued with us in the church. This raised a great excitement and inquiry among the citizens, in so much that I believe they were ashamed of their conduct. But my dear Lord was with us, and we were filled with fresh vigour to get a house erected to worship God in ★

THE AUTHOR

A leading abolitionist, Richard Allen was the African Methodist Episcopal Church's first bishop. He was president of the first national black convention held in 1830 and founder of a school for African-American children and adults.

Allen bought his freedom after convincing his master to let him and his brother hire themselves out at night and on weekends to make money to do so. Already a converted Methodist, Allen traveled preaching to anyone who would listen. After arriving in Philadelphia, he remained there until he died in 1831. A dedicated and tireless worker for his people, Allen earned the title of a Founding Father of black America.

THE RESPONSE

Richard Allen and Absalom Jones had already organized the Free African Society of Philadelphia some months before they walked out of St. George's Church. After leaving the church, they held worship service at the society. There they made plans to establish their own place of worship. In 1794 two churches emerged from this organization. First, the African Episcopal Church of St. Thomas was formed under Absalom Jones. A few months later, Richard Allen purchased property in Philadelphia and had an old building he bought moved to the site. There, his church, Bethel African Methodist Episcopal, began.

We wish to plead
our own cause.
Too long
have others spoken for us.

—John Russwurm

SAMUEL B. CORNISH 1795–1858

JOHN RUSSWURM 1799–1851

African Americans continued to form their own churches, institutions, and organizations. Baptist churches were among the first African-American institutions in America. George Liele and Andrew Bryan led this movement in the South. Thomas Paul and Josiah Bishop were leaders in the North. In 1787 Richard Allen and Absalom Jones organized the Free African Society. Later that year, Prince Hall organized African Lodge No. 459, the first African-American Masonic Order. He also helped to organize lodges in other cities. In 1794 Allen and Jones started their own churches. Year by year, African Americans in all parts of the country organized themselves to look after their own interests.

In 1827 two young African Americans published the first black newspaper in America. In the editorial in the first edition of *Freedom's Journal*, they expressed why they took such a monumental step.

t is our earnest wish to make our Journal a medium of intercourse between our brethren in the different states of this great confederacy: that through its columns an expression of our sentiments, on many interesting subjects which concern us, may be offered to the publick; that plans which apparently are beneficial may be candidly discussed and properly weighed; if worth, receive our cordial approbation; if not, our marked disapprobation.

Useful knowledge of every kind, and everything that relates to Africa, shall find a ready admission into our columns; and as that vast continent becomes daily more known, we trust that many things will come to light, proving that the natives of it are neither so ignorant nor stupid as they have generally been supposed to be.

And while these important subjects shall occupy the columns of the FREEDOM'S JOURNAL, we would not be unmindful of our brethren who are still in the iron fetters of bondage. They are kindred by all the times of nature; and though but little can be effected by us, still let our sympathies be poured forth, and our prayers in their behalf, ascend to Him who is able to succour them.

From the press and the pulpit we have suffered much by being incorrectly represented. Men whom we equally love and admire have not hesitated to represent us disadvantageously, without becoming personally acquainted with the true state of things, nor discerning between virtue and vice among us. The virtuous part of our people feel themselves sorely aggrieved under the existing state of things—they are not appreciated ★

THE AUTHOR

Samuel E. Cornish and John B. Russwurm were young leaders of the New York City black community. Both lived as free men. Cornish was born in Delaware around 1795 and resided in Philadelphia and New York City. He was a minister and helped to organize the first African-American Presbyterian church in New York City. Russwurm was born in Jamaica of mixed parentage. His white father sent him to school in Canada. A graduate of Bowdoin College in 1826, he was among the first African-American college graduates.

Cornish worked with a number of publications after *Freedom's Journal*. Russwurm became a supporter of the Back to Africa Movement and later moved to Liberia, where he died in 1851.

THE RESPONSE

African Americans in all sections of the country encouraged and supported *Freedom's Journal*. Published every Friday for two years, it highlighted achievements by African Americans and served as a forum for protest. Equally important, it presented African Americans as human beings. During this period, many whites felt African Americans were less than human.

Cornish and Russwurm's publication gave birth to the black press. By the time the Civil War began in 1861, there were twenty-four African-American newspapers and a number of magazines and periodicals being published in America.

"They think because they hold us in infernal chains we wish to be white, or of their color, but they are dreadfully deceived— we wish to be just as it pleased our Creator to have made us."

—David Walker

From *Walker's Appeal in Four Articles to the Colored Citizens of the World, but in Particular, and very Expressly, to Those of the United States of America* ⋆ 1829

DAVID WALKER

1785–1830

David Walker had grown tired of waiting for slavery to end. Slaveholders, he believed, would never be convinced that slavery was wrong. They had too much to lose. Walker felt the time had come for slaves to fight for their freedom. So he published a pamphlet to get his view out to the public, especially to African-American slaves. Commonly called *David Walker's Appeal*, the pamphlet caused fear all across the country.

But slavery in America continued to grow at a rapid rate. In 1800 there were nearly 900,000 slaves. In 1820 the number had increased to more than 1½ million. In 1830, a year after Walker's pamphlet was published, there were two million slaves in America.

I am fully aware, in making this appeal to my much afflicted and suffering brethren, that I shall not only be assailed by those whose greatest earthly desires are, to keep us in abject ignorance and wretchedness, and who are of the firm conviction that Heaven has designed us and our children to be slaves and *beasts of burden* to them and their children. I say, I do not only expect to be held up to the public as an ignorant impudent and restless disturber of the public peace, by such avaricious creatures, as well as a mover of insubordination—and perhaps put in prison or to death, for giving a superficial exposition of our miseries and exposing tyrants. But I am persuaded, that many of my brethren, particularly those who are ignorantly in league with slave-holders or tyrants, who acquire their daily bread by the blood and sweat of their more ignorant brethren—and not a few of those too, who are too ignorant to see an inch beyond their noses, will rise up and call me cursed—Yea, the jealous ones among us will perhaps use more abject subtlety, by affirming that this work is not worth perusing, that we are well situated, that there is no use in trying to better our condition, for we cannot. I will ask one question here.—Can our condition be any worse?—Can it be more mean and abject? If there are any changes will they not be for the better, though they may appear for the worst at first? Can they get us any lower? Where can they get us? They are afraid to treat us worse, for they know well, the day they do it they are gone. But against all accusations which may or can be

preferred against me, I appeal to Heaven for my motive in writing—who knows that my object is, if possible, to awaken in the breasts of my afflicted, degraded and slumbering brethren, a spirit of inquiry and investigation respecting our miseries and wretchedness in this REPUBLICAN LAND OF LIBERTY!!!!!!

The sources from which our miseries are derived, and on which I shall comment, I shall not combine in one, but shall put them under distinct heads and expose them in their turn; in doing which, keeping truth on my side and not departing from the strictest rules of morality, I shall endeavour to penetrate, search out, and lay them open for your inspection. If you cannot or will not profit by them, I shall have done *my* duty to you, my country and my God ★

THE AUTHOR

David Walker was born in 1785 in North Carolina. His father, a slave, died before he was born. He was raised by his mother, a free black woman. Walker eventually settled in Boston, where he was an organizer, and a member of a black abolitionist group. His home was a refuge for African Americans in need, especially those who had escaped from slavery. He was also an agent for *Freedom's Journal.*

After the publication of his *Appeal,* Walker became a target of slavery supporters. When he was found dead in 1830, his supporters thought he had been poisoned by someone who supported slavery.

THE RESPONSE

The release of *Walker's Appeal* caused an uproar in America, especially in the South. Slave owners felt that the sixty-four-page pamphlet would incite slaves to rebel. Several states began enacting additional laws to tighten their control over slaves.

Walker's Appeal charted a new course for some African Americans by urging armed rebellion to fight slavery. Walker also identified African Americans with the greatness of Egypt and the rest of Africa. He ushered in the militant movement for African-American freedom in America.

Dred Scott's Petition to Sue for His Freedom • JULY 1847

DRED SCOTT

1799–1858

The struggle against slavery was carried out in many different ways. There were rebellions. There were organized efforts that helped escaped slaves to freedom. There was pressure put on lawmakers to get them to change laws. In 1847 Dred Scott attempted to obtain his freedom through the legal system. After nine years, his case made it all the way to the United States Supreme Court. Scott's lawyer argued that because Scott had lived in Illinois, a state where slavery was not legal, he was entitled to his freedom. His master had taken him from Illinois to Missouri, a slave state, to live. The ruling the Supreme Court rendered in 1857 was one of the most important decisions in the history of the court.

A majority opinion said that African Americans were "so far inferior that they had no rights which a white man was bound to respect." Slaves were already considered property, and without rights as citizens. Now, because of this decision, it did not matter whether an African American lived in a slave state or a free state, or if he was enslaved or free; he could not be regarded as a citizen of the United States. The decision pushed the country closer to war.

our petitioner, Dred Scott, a man of color, respectfully represents that sometime in the year 1835 your petitioner was purchased as a slave by one John Emerson, since deceased, who afterwards, to-wit; about the year 1836 or 1837, conveyed your petitioner from the State of Missouri to Fort Snelling, a fort then occupied by the troops of the United States and under the jurisdiction of the United States, situated in the territory ceded by France to the United States under the name of Louisiana, lying north of 36 degrees and 30′ North latitude, now included in the State of Missouri, and resided and continued to reside at Fort Snelling upwards of one year, and held your petitioner in slavery at such Fort during all that time in violation of the Act of Congress of 1806 and 1820, entitled An Act to Authorize the People of Missouri Territory to form a Constitution and State Government, and for the admission of such State into the Union on an equal footing with the original states, and to Prohibit Slavery in Certain Territories.

Your petitioner avers that said Emerson has since departed this life, leaving his widow and an infant whose name is unknown to your petitioner; and that one Alexander Sandford administered upon the estate of said Emerson and that our petitioner is now unlawfully held in slavery by said Sandford and by said administrator and said Irene Emerson claims your petitioner as part of the estate of said Emerson and by one Samuel Russell.

Your petitioner therefore prays your Honorable Court to grant him leave to sue as a poor person, in order to establish his right to freedom, and that the necessary orders may be made in the premises ⋆

THE AUTHOR

Dred Scott, born in Virginia around 1799, was taken to Missouri in 1830 by his owners. He was then sold to Dr. John Emerson, a military surgeon. Dr. Emerson and Scott spent the next twelve years traveling to military posts in Illinois and the Wisconsin Territory. During this time Scott married Harriett Robinson, who was also a slave. She was purchased by Dr. Emerson.

In 1842 Dr. Emerson returned to Missouri. A year later he died. In 1846 Scott and his wife sued Dr. Emerson's widow, claiming that because they had lived in free states they should be declared free. The suit began an eleven-year quest for freedom by the Scotts. After Mrs. Emerson remarried, she returned Scott to his original owners because her new husband opposed slavery. The Scotts were then given their freedom. Dred Scott died a year later.

THE RESPONSE

In the Dred Scott decision, the Supreme Court ruled that African Americans, both enslaved and free, were not regarded as citizens by the United States Constitution. In addition, it ruled that congressional legislation that prohibited slavery in new territories entering the union was unconstitutional.

The decision was a major blow to the antislavery movement. It intensified the growing division of opinion concerning slavery in the United States. Abolitionists, both black and white, redoubled their antislavery efforts. Many feared it would take war to end the institution that had been a part of America for two hundred years.

An Address to the Ohio Women's Rights Convention ★ MAY 29, 1851

SOJOURNER TRUTH

1797–1883

The most effective abolitionist speakers were ex-slaves. They knew the awful conditions of bondage. They knew the pain and suffering slaves had to endure. They, too, had felt the lash. They, too, had seen their mothers, fathers, and siblings sold away. Many still had relatives and friends in slavery. No one could capture the horrors of servitude like the ex-slave.

Sojourner Truth was an ex-slave. She escaped from slavery in 1826, but didn't begin her crusade for freedom until 1843. Antislavery speakers often faced cruel and vicious mobs. Sojourner Truth was even more of a target because she was a woman. But she faced the challenges boldly and courageously during a long career dedicated to freedom and equal rights.

ell, children, where there is so much racket there must be somethin' out o' kilter. I think that 'twixt the Negroes in the North and the South and the women at the North, all talkin' 'bout rights, the white men will be in a fix pretty soon. But what's all this here talkin' 'bout?

That man over there say that women needs to be helped into carriages, and lifted over ditches, and to have the best place everywhere. Nobody ever helps me into carriages, or over mud-puddles, or give me any best place! And ain't I a woman? Look at me? Look at my arm? I have ploughed, and planted, and gathered into barns, and no man could head me! And ain't I a woman? I could work as much and eat as much as a man—when I could get it—and bear the lash as well! And ain't I a woman? I have borne thirteen children, and seen 'em mos' all sold off to slavery, and when I cried out with my mother's grief, none but Jesus heard me! And ain't I a woman?

Then they talk about this thing in the head; what's this they call it? [*"Intellect," whispered some one near.*] That's it honey. What's that got to do with women's rights or Negro rights? If my cup won't hold but a pint and yours holds a quart, wouldn't you be mean not to let me have my little half measure full?

Then that little man in black there, he says women can't have as much rights as men, 'cause Christ wasn't a woman!

"I CAN'T READ A BOOK, BUT I CAN READ PEOPLE."
—Sojourner Truth

Where did your Christ come from? Where did your Christ come from? From God and a woman! Man had nothin' to do with Him.

If the first woman God ever made was strong enough to turn the world upside down all alone, these women together ought to be able to turn it back and get it right side up again? And now they is asking to do it, they better let 'em. 'Bliged to you for hearin' me, and now ole Sojourner hasn't got nothin' more to say ⋆

THE AUTHOR

Sojourner Truth was the first African-American woman to gain national recognition as an antislavery speaker. Born into slavery around 1797 in Hurley, New York, she was given the name Isabella Baumfree. While a youngster, Sojourner was sold to several different masters. In 1826 she ran away from her last master, leaving her husband and children. In 1843 she left New York City, where she had been living, and began to travel. She changed her name to Sojourner Truth because she believed she had received a vision from God telling her to travel and spread the truth. From 1843 until her death in 1883, Sojourner Truth dedicated her life to the struggle of freedom for African Americans and equal rights for women.

THE RESPONSE

Organizers of the women's rights convention in Ohio hadn't scheduled Sojourner Truth as a speaker. Some of them felt that the cause of women's rights would be jeopardized if it were aligned with the antislavery movement.

As the convention continued, opponents of women's rights threatened to disrupt the event. They ridiculed and laughed at participants. Sojourner couldn't stand by any longer. As she walked slowly onto the stage, some of the women's rights supporters chanted to prevent her from speaking. But Sojourner was allowed to speak. By the time she finished, the jeers and protests had turned into cheers. Those in the women's rights movement now knew they had a powerful ally in Sojourner Truth.

"The white man's happiness cannot be purchased by the black man's misery."

—Frederick Douglass

From a Speech Given to the Rochester Antislavery Sewing
Society, Rochester, New York ★ JULY 4, 1852

FREDERICK DOUGLASS

1817–1895

By 1850 there were more than three million African Americans held in slavery. And the more than 400,000 free African Americans faced discrimination daily. That same year, the Fugitive Slave Act, which declared that slaves who escaped to nonslave states must be returned to their masters, was passed by Congress. The end of slavery and discrimination in America seemed far, far away.

Like many other African Americans, Frederick Douglass had become more militant in his views. While most white abolitionists favored passive resistance, Douglass and other black abolitionists called for the ballot, if possible; the bullet, if necessary. His Fourth of July speech expressed the frustration he felt about the worsening plight of African Americans.

t a time like this, scorching irony, not convincing argument, is needed. O! had I the ability, and could reach the nation's ear, I would, today, pour out a fiery stream of biting ridicule, blasting reproach, withering sarcasm and stern rebuke. For it is not light that is needed, but fire; it is not the gentle shower, but thunder. We need the storm, the whirlwind, and the earthquake. The feeling of the nation must be quickened; the conscience of the nation must be roused; the propriety of the nation must be startled; the hypocrisy of the nation must be exposed; and its crimes against God and man must be proclaimed and denounced.

What, to the American slave, is your Fourth of July? I answer: a day that reveals to him, more than all other days of the year, the gross injustice and cruelty to which he is the constant victim. To him, your celebration is a sham; your boasted liberty an unholy license; your national greatness swelling vanity; your sounds of rejoicing are empty and heartless; your denunciation of tyrants brass-fronted impudence; your shouts of liberty and equality hollow mockery; your prayers and hymns, your sermons and thanksgivings, with all your religious parade and solemnity, are to Him mere bombast, fraud, deception, impiety and hypocrisy—a thin veil to cover up crimes which would disgrace a nation of savages. There is not a nation on the earth guilty of practices more shocking and bloody than are the people of the United States at this very hour.

Go where you may, search where you will, roam through all the monarchies and despotism of the Old World, travel through South America, search out every abuse, and when you have found the last, lay your facts by the side of the everyday practices of this nation, and you will say with me, that, for revolting barbarity and shameless hypocrisy, America reigns without a rival ⋆

THE AUTHOR

Frederick Douglass was born in 1817 on the eastern shore of Maryland. At the age of twenty-one he escaped from his master and made his way to New Bedford, Massachusetts, where he became a member of the abolitionist movement. In 1841 William Lloyd Garrison, a leading abolitionist, heard Douglass speak and was so impressed with his speaking ability that he and members of the Massachusetts Anti-Slavery Society hired Douglass as a lecturer. Douglass soon became one of the antislavery movement's leading spokesmen.

After slavery ended, Douglass continued his role as one of the most important, and most recognized, African-American leaders of his time. During his later years, he served in a number of federal positions.

THE RESPONSE

When Frederick Douglass published his autobiography in 1845, he had to flee to England. His former owner sought to capture and enslave him again. Friends in England purchased his freedom for $150. Prior to leaving for England, Douglass had worked for the Massachusetts Anti-Slavery Society for six years. From the beginning, whites had played the leading roles in the antislavery movement. African Americans such as Douglass were used to give a face to slavery with their speeches. Douglass felt African Americans should be part of the abolitionist leadership. They had the most to gain and to lose. When he returned to America from England, he had already decided to strike out on his own. Douglass moved to Rochester, New York, and began publishing the *North Star*, his own antislavery newspaper, and continued to develop his own views about the problems that the country faced. He was now an African-American leader and not just an antislavery lecturer.

"Bury Me in a Free Land" From the Book
Poems on Miscellaneous Subjects ⋆ 1854

FRANCES ELLEN WATKINS HARPER

1825–1911

In many states it was against the law to teach slaves to read and write. But many learned anyway. Free African Americans viewed education as crucial in the struggle for freedom and equality.

Many African Americans used the written word to bring attention to the antislavery cause. Their works helped to get the antislavery message to a greater number of people. They included David Walker, Samuel B. Cornish, John Russwurm, Frederick Douglass, Harriet Jacobs, William Wells, and Frances W. Harper.

Frances Harper was the most widely published of all African-American writers of the nineteenth century. Many of her poems, articles, and essays were featured in the leading publications of the time.

Make me aggrieve
where'er you will,
In a lowly plain, or a lofty hill;
Make it among earth's humblest graves,
But not in a land where men are slaves.

I could not rest if around my grave
I heard the steps of a trembling slave;
His shadow above my silent tomb
Would make it a place of fearful gloom.

I could not rest if I heard the tread
of a coffle gang to the shambles led,
And the mother's shriek of wild despair
Rise like a curse on the trembling air.

I could not sleep, if I saw the lash
Drinking her blood at each fearful gash,
And I saw her babes torn from her breast,
Like trembling doves from their parent nest.

I'd shudder and start if I heard the bay
of bloodhounds seizing their human prey,
And I heard the captive plead in vain
As they bound afresh his galling chain.

"AND WHAT IS WRONG IN A WOMAN'S LIFE IN A MAN'S CANNOT BE RIGHT."
—*Frances Ellen Watkins Harper*

If I saw young girls from their mother's arms
bartered and sold for their youthful charms,
My eye would flash with a mournful flame,
My death-paled cheek grow red with shame

I would sleep, dear friends, where bloated might
Can rob no man of his dearest right;
My rest shall be calm in any grave
Where none can call his brother a slave.

I ask no monument, proud and high,
To arrest the gaze of the passers-by;
All that my yearning spirit craves,
Is bury me not in a land of slaves! ★

THE AUTHOR

Frances Ellen Watkins Harper was a writer, teacher, lecturer, abolitionist, and women's rights activist. She was born in Baltimore, Maryland, in 1825. Her parents, both of whom were free, died when she was very young. So she was sent to live with an uncle who taught at a school for African-American children.

Harper began writing poetry when she was a teenager. Her first poems were published in abolitionist periodicals. In 1851 she published her first collection of poems, entitled *Forest Leaves.* During the 1850s she became active in the Underground Railroad. She soon began to tour as an anti-slavery speaker. Harper continued to lecture and write about the condition of African Americans and women until her death in 1911.

THE RESPONSE

"Bury Me in a Free Land" first appeared in a collection of poems entitled *Poems on Miscellaneous Subjects,* published in 1854. The collection sold 10,000 copies in five years. The poem was also published in antislavery periodicals. It was featured in William Lloyd Garrison's *Liberator* in 1864.

Frances Harper wrote novels, articles, and essays as well as poetry. Her writing appeared in many publications during her long career. She is best remembered for her poetry, however. Harper is generally considered to have ushered in the African-American tradition of protest poetry.

"The time has come when you must act for yourselves."

—Henry Highland Garnet

From a Speech Delivered in the Hall of the United States
House of Representatives ★ FEBRUARY 12, 1865

HENRY HIGHLAND GARNET

1815–1882

On January 31, 1865, the United States House of Representatives passed a new amendment to the Constitution. If ratified by the required number of states, the amendment would end slavery in the United States. President Abraham Lincoln had issued the Emancipation Proclamation in 1863. But it only ended slavery in states that were at war against the Union. The new amendment, the 14th, would end slavery in the entire country.

The noted African-American abolitionist Henry Highland Garnet was in the gallery that January 31. Like all those assembled that historic day, Garnet was filled with joy. A long struggle had finally ended victoriously. A few weeks later, garnet delivered an impassioned speech before Congress in which he expressed the importance of the new amendment to African Americans.

onorable Senators and Representatives! illustrious rulers of this great nation! I cannot refrain this day from invoking upon you, in God's name, the blessings of millions who were ready to perish, but to whom a new and better life has been opened by your humanity, justice and patriotism. You have said, "Let the Constitution of the country be so amended that slavery and involuntary servitude shall no longer exist in the United States, except in punishment for crime." Surely, an act so sublime could not escape Divine notice; and doubtless the deed has been recorded in the archives of heaven. Volumes may be appropriated to your praise and reknown in the history of the world. Genius and art may perpetuate the glorious act on canvas and in marble, but certain and more lasting monuments in commemoration of your decision are already erected in the hearts and memories of a grateful people.

The nation has begun its exodus from worse than Egyptian bondage; and I beseech you that you say to the people, *"that they go forward."* With the assurance of God's favor in all things done in obedience to his righteous will, and guided by day and by night by the pillars of cloud and fire, let us not pause until we have reached the other and safe side of the stormy and crimson sea. Let freemen and patriots mete out complete and equal justice to all men, and thus prove to mankind the superiority of our Democratic, Republican Government ⋆

THE AUTHOR

Henry Highland Garnet was a leading antislavery crusader and a minister. Along with Frederick Douglass, Garnet was considered to be the most prominent African-American leader during the abolitionist movement. Garnet was more militant than Douglass.

Born into slavery in 1815 in Maryland, Garnet escaped with his parents to Pennsylvania when he was nine. He was ordained a Presbyterian minister and served as a pastor in a number of churches in New York State and Washington, D.C. He was noted for his rousing, eloquent speeches against slavery.

THE RESPONSE

Some slaves had obtained their freedom as a result of the Emancipation Proclamation. But the majority were still held in bondage. So the passage of the Thirteenth Amendment brought great excitement to those who had carried on a long and determined struggle to end slavery. Garnet's speech before Congress captured that excitement. He had been invited to speak as a part of the anniversary celebration of the signing of the Emancipation Proclamation. He was the first African American to speak before Congress. On December 18, 1865, after the required number of states had approved it, the Thirteenth Amendment became a part of the United States Constitution.

"I have confidence not only in my country and her institutions but in the endurance, capacity and destiny of my people."

—Blanche K. Bruce

**From a Speech to the United States Senate
on the Mississippi Election** ★ MARCH 31, 1876

BLANCHE K.
1841–1898
BRUCE

Following the Civil War, a number of laws and amendments were passed to help newly freed slaves adjust to freedom and to ensure their equality before the law. Among them were the Fourteenth and Fifteenth amendments, which made African Americans citizens and gave them the right to vote. During this period, called Reconstruction (1865–1877), African Americans held political offices in state and local government. Some owned businesses. Many people believed that African Americans were moving rapidly to achieve equality in the South. But that optimism would soon fade, as Southern whites gained power once again. Blanche K. Bruce of Mississippi delivered this speech concerning the plight of African Americans in his state to his colleagues in the United States Senate.

he conduct of the late election in Mississippi affected not merely the fortunes of the partisans—as the same were necessarily involved in the defeat or success of the respective parties to the contest—but put in question and jeopardy the sacred rights of the citizens; and the investigation contemplated in the pending resolution has for its object not the determination of the question whether the offices shall be held and the public affairs of the State be administered by democrats or republicans, but the higher and more important end, the protection in all their purity and significance of the political rights of the people and the free institutions of the country.

The evidence in hand and accessible will show beyond peradventure that in many parts of the State corrupt and violent influences were brought to bear upon the registrars of voters, thus materially affecting the character of the voting or poll lists; upon the inspectors of election, prejudicially and unfairly, thereby changing the number of votes cast; and finally threats and violence were practiced directly upon the masses of voters in such measures and strength as to produce grave apprehensions for personal safety and as to deter them from the exercise of their political franchises.

It will not accord with the laws of nature or history to brand colored people a race of cowards. On more than one historic field, beginning in 1776 and coming down to the centennial year of the Republic, they have attested in blood their courage as well as a love of liberty. I ask Senators to believe that no consideration of fear or personal danger has kept us quiet and forbearing under the provocations and wrongs that have so sorely tried our souls. But feeling kindly towards our white fellow-citizens, appreciating the good purposes and offices of the better classes, and, above all, abhorring war of races, we determined to wait until such time as an appeal to the good sense and justice of the American people can be made ★

THE AUTHOR

Blanche K. Bruce was born a slave in Farmville, Virginia, in 1841. His family later moved to Missouri, where he received his formal education. He then studied at Oberlin College in Ohio. After moving back to Mississippi following the Civil War, Bruce worked as a planter and entered politics. He held a number of local offices, then was elected to the United States Senate in 1875, becoming the first African American to serve a complete six-year term.

THE RESPONSE

In 1875, when Blanche K. Bruce delivered his speech before the U.S. Senate, the struggle for equality was quickly losing ground. The national resolve to protect African Americans' rights had waned. Southern whites were beginning to seize power again. With that power came laws that stripped African Americans of their rights. If laws worked too slowly, violence and intimidation were used. Soon, a new system was instituted to replace slavery. It was called segregation. The dream of equality for the African American had turned into a nightmare.

From *A Red Record* ⋆ 1895

IDA B. WELLS 1862–1931
BARNETT

It didn't take long for whites to reestablish a system of racial oppression in the South after Reconstruction ended. State and local governments headed by whites enacted thousands of laws designed to deny African Americans their rights as citizens. These laws, called "Jim Crow Laws" after a pre–Civil War minstrel character, established two separate and unequal societies, one white and one black.

Whites used all forms of intimidation to keep this system in place. African Americans were jailed, beaten, and killed. Lynching was a favorite method, in which they were routinely hanged by whites without a trial. A close friend of Ida B. Wells Barnett was a victim. Angered and determined, Barnett launched a vigorous campaign to bring attention to this horrible practice. *A Red Record* is one of the pamphlets she published.

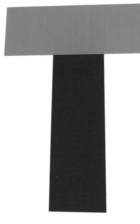he student of American sociology will find the year 1894 marked by a pronounced awakening of the public conscience to a system of anarchy and outlawry which has grown during a series of ten years to be so common, that scenes of unusual brutality failed to have any visible effect upon the humane sentiments of the people of our land.

Beginning with the emancipation of the Negro, the inevitable result of unbridled power exercised for two and a half centuries, by the white man over the Negro, began to show itself in acts of conscienceless outlawry. During the slave regime, the Southern white man owned the Negro body and soul. It was to his interest to dwarf the soul and preserve the body. Vested with unlimited power over his slave, to subject him to any and all kinds of physical punishment, the white man was still restrained from such punishment as tended to injure the slave by abating his physical powers and thereby reducing his financial worth. While slaves were scourged mercilessly, and in countless cases inhumanly treated in other respects, still the white owner rarely permitted his anger to go so far as to take a life, which would entail upon him a loss of several hundred dollars. The slave was rarely killed, he was too valuable; it was easier and quite as effective, for the discipline or revenge, to sell him "Down South."

But Emancipation came and the vested interests of the

white man in the Negro's body were lost. The white man had no right to scourge the emancipated Negro, still less has he a right to kill him. But the Southern white people had been educated so long in that school of practice, in which might makes right, that they disdained to draw strict lines of action in dealing with the Negro. In slave times the Negro was kept subservient and submissive by the frequency and severity of the scourging, but, with freedom, a new system of intimidation came in vogue; the Negro was not only whipped and scourged; he was killed.

Not all nor nearly all of the murders done by white men, during the past thirty years in the South, have come to light, but the statistics are gathered and preserved by white men, and which have not been questioned, show that during these years more than ten thousand Negroes have been killed in cold blood, without the formality of judicial trial or legal execution. And yet, as evidence of the absolute impunity with which the white man dare to kill a Negro, the same record shows that during all these years, and for all these murders only three white men have been tried, convicted, and executed. As no white man has been lynched for the murder of colored people, these three executions are the only instances of the death penalty being visited upon white men for murdering Negroes.

Naturally enough the commission of these crimes began to tell upon the public conscience, and the Southern white man, as a tribute to the nineteenth-century civilization, was

"THREATS CANNOT SUPPRESS THE TRUTH."
—Ida B. Wells Barnett

in a manner compelled to give excuses for his barbarism. His excuses have adapted themselves to the emergency, and are aptly outlined by that greatest of all Negroes, Frederick Douglass, in an article of recent date, in which he shows that there have been three distinct eras of Southern barbarism, to account for which three distinct excuses have been made.

The first excuse given to the civilized world for the murder of unoffending Negroes was the necessity of the white men to repress and stamp out alleged "race riots." For years immediately succeeding the war there was an appalling slaughter of colored people, and the wires usually conveyed to Northern people and the world the intelligence, first, that an insurrection was being planned by Negroes, which, a few hours later, would prove to have been vigorously resisted and wounded. It was always a remarkable feature in these insurrections and riots that only Negroes were killed during the rioting, and that all the white men escaped unharmed ✶

THE AUTHOR

Ida B. Wells Barnett's early career was as a schoolteacher. Born in Mississippi during the Civil War, she starting teaching to help support her five brothers and sisters when their parents died from yellow fever. Barnett began writing about the plight of African Americans for local newspapers after she moved to Memphis, Tennessee. Soon she was writing for African-American newspapers around the country. She began her antilynching crusade in 1892 when Tom Moss, a close friend, was lynched. For years, Barnett was in the forefront of the African-American struggle for equality and justice.

THE RESPONSE

Following the death of her friend, Ida Barnett began writing articles about the lynching of African Americans. She compiled and examined scores of cases and found that 728 African-American men and women had been lynched in a ten-year period. In addition to writing articles and pamphlets, Barnett spoke to groups and organizations around the country and in England. She lobbied Congress to enact antilynching legislation. Her efforts motivated others to speak out. The number of cases decreased for a few years, but the lynching of African Americans continued. Barnett reported in a speech in 1909 to the founding conference of the National Association for the Advancement of Colored People that 3,284 people had been lynched during the prior quarter of the century.

"Lynching
is the aftermath of
slavery."

—Mary Church Terrell

MARY CHURCH TERRELL

1863–1954

The early leaders of the women's rights movement began their reform efforts in the antislavery movement. Elizabeth Cady Stanton, Susan B. Anthony, and Lucretia Mott, leaders of the feminist movement, were all abolitionists. African-American women such as Harriett Tubman, Sojourner Truth, and Frances Ellen Harper lent their voices to the cause of women's rights. They faced discrimination and prejudice because of their race and because of their sex. Most of these dedicated, courageous women, however, considered the struggle for African-American equality paramount. Yet they recognized that their rights as women must also be secured. Mary Church Terrell was a leader in both struggles.

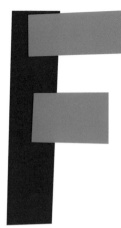ifty years ago a meeting such as this, planned, conducted and addressed by women would have been an impossibility. Less than forty years ago, few sane men would have predicted that either a slave or one of his descendants would in this century at least, address such an audience in the Nation's Capital at the invitation of women representing the highest, broadest, best type of womanhood, that can be found anywhere in the world.

Thus to me this semi-centennial of the National American Woman Suffrage Association is a double jubilee, rejoicing as I do, not only in the prospective enfranchisement of my sex but in the emancipation of my race. When Ernestine Rose, Lucretia Mott, Elizabeth Cady Stanton, Lucy Stone, and Susan B. Anthony began that agitation by which colleges were opened to women and the numerous reforms inaugurated for the amelioration of their condition along all lines, their sisters who groaned in bondage had little reason to hope that these blessings would ever brighten their crushed and blighted lives, for during those days of oppression and despair, colored women were not only refused admittance to institutions of learning, but the law of the United States in which the majority lived made it a crime to teach them to read. Not only could they possess no property, but even their bodies were not their own. Nothing, in short, that could degrade or brutalize the womanhood of the race was lacking in that system from which colored women then had little hope of escape. So gloomy were their prospects, so fatal the laws, so pernicious the customs, only fifty years ago.

But, from the day their fetters were broken and their minds released from the darkness of ignorance to which for more than two hundred years they had been doomed from the day they could stand erect in the dignity of womanhood, no longer bond but free, till tonight, colored women have forged steadily ahead in the acquisition of knowledge and in the cultivation of those virtues which make for good. To use a thought of the illustrious Frederick Douglass, if judged by the depths from which they have come, rather than by the heights to which those blessed with centuries of opportunities have attained, colored women need not hang their heads in shame.

Consider if you will, the almost insurmountable obstacles which have confronted colored women in their efforts to educate and cultivate themselves since their emancipation, and I dare assert, not boastfully, but with pardonable pride, I hope, that the progress they have made and the work they have accomplished, will bear a favorable comparison at least with that of their more fortunate sisters, from the opportunity of acquiring knowledge and the means of self-culture have never been entirely withheld. For, not only are colored women with ambition and aspiration handicapped on account of their sex, but they are everywhere baffled and mocked on account of their race. Desperately and continuously they are forced to fight that opposition, born of cruel, unreasonable prejudice which neither their merit nor their necessity seems able to subdue. Not only because they are women, but because they are colored women, are discouragement and disappointment meeting them at every turn.

. . . And so, lifting as we climb, onward and upward we go, struggling and striving, and hoping that the buds and blossoms of our desires will burst into glorious fruition ere long. With courage, born of success achieved in the past, with a keen sense of the responsibility which we shall continue to assume, we look forward to a future large with promise and hope. Seeking no favors because of our color, nor patronage because of our needs, we knock at the bar of justice, asking an equal chance ★

THE AUTHOR

Because Mary Church Terrell's father was a successful businessman, she lived a life of privilege. She attended the best schools, including Oberlin College in Ohio from which she graduated in 1884. Later she embarked upon a career as a teacher. In 1892 Tom Moss, a childhood friend who was also a friend of Ida B. Wells Barnett, was lynched in Memphis, Tennessee. Saddened and angered, Mary joined the struggle for equality and justice for African Americans and for women. She quickly became a leader and spent the remainder of her life committed to that struggle.

THE RESPONSE

Mary Church Terrell was often asked to speak at women's rights conferences. She always used the opportunities to shed light on the plight of African Americans. She recognized that African-American women would not necessarily enjoy rights won by the movement. This was proved when the Nineteenth Amendment, which gave women the right to vote, was ratified in 1920. Although African-American women had picketed and protested for the passage of the amendment, in most places in the South they still were not allowed to vote.

From a Speech Delivered at the Cotton State and
International Exposition, Atlanta, Georgia · 1895

BOOKER T. 1856–1915
WASHINGTON

As the 1800s neared an end, the major problem facing African Americans was how to achieve first-class citizenship. The dream of full citizenship that followed the Civil War had faded. Ex-slaveholders, former Confederate soldiers, and racists had restored white supremacy in the South. Racial segregation had been well established in other parts of the country, too.

Of the different approaches to achieving first-class citizenship, two were most accepted by the majority of African Americans. Booker T. Washington was the leader of one approach. Washington believed that if African Americans became skilled workers, they could eventually prove their worth and then gain their equal rights as citizens. He urged African Americans not to fight for equal rights; instead, he encouraged them to concentrate on building their own businesses and communities.

That approach was first presented on a national scale in a speech delivered at the Cotton State and International Exposition in Atlanta. Most of white America supported Booker T. Washington, who soon became the most powerful African American in the country.

A ship lost at sea for many days suddenly sighted a friendly vessel. From the mast of the unfortunate vessel was seen a signal: "Water, water; we die of thirst!" The answer from the friendly vessel at once came back: "Cast down your bucket where you are." A second time the signal, "Water, water, send us water!" ran up from the distressed vessel, and was answered: "Cast down your bucket where you are." And a third and fourth signal for water was answered: "Cast down your bucket where you are." The captain of the distressed vessel, at last heeding the injunction, cast down his bucket, and it came up full of fresh, sparkling water from the mouth of the Amazon River. To those of my race who depend on bettering their condition in a foreign land, or who underestimate the importance of cultivating friendly relations with the Southern white man, who is their next door neighbor, I would say: "Cast down your bucket where you are"—cast it down in making friends in every manly way of the people of all races by whom we are surrounded.

Cast it down in agriculture, mechanics, in commerce, in domestic service, and in the professions. And in this connection it is well to bear in mind that whatever other sins the South may be called to bear, when it comes to business, pure and simple, it is in the South that the Negro is given a man's chance in the commercial world, and in nothing is this Exposition more eloquent than in emphasizing this chance.

"AN INCH OF PROGRESS IS WORTH A YARD OF COMPLAINT."
—Booker T. Washington

Our greatest danger is that in the great leap from slavery to freedom we may overlook the fact that the masses of us are to live by the productions of our hands, and fail to keep in mind that we shall prosper in proportion as we learn to dignify and glorify common labor, and put brains and skill into the common occupations of life; shall prosper in proportion as we learn to draw the line between the superficial and the substantial, the ornamental gewgaws of life and the useful. No race can prosper till it learns that there is as much dignity in tilling a field as in writing a poem. It is at the bottom of life we must begin, and not at the top. Nor should we permit our grievances to overshadow our opportunities ★

THE AUTHOR

Booker T. Washington was an educator and the most influential African American of his day. Born into slavery, he was freed during the Civil War. After graduating from Hampton Institute and teaching there for a while, he founded Tuskegee Institute in 1881. At Tuskegee he stressed industrial education rather than academics, and was able to secure the support of influential whites. The school soon became the leading African-American institution of higher learning in America. In 1900 Washington founded the National Negro Business League. Presidents and government officials sought his advice and approval concerning issues related to African Americans.

THE RESPONSE

Tuskegee Institute specialized in agricultural and industrial training. As the principal at Tuskegee Institute, Booker T. Washington prepared his students for careers in trade and taught them to accept their "second-class" status. This was the approach to the country's race problem that he presented at the Atlanta Exposition. He quickly gained public attention, especially from white America. Money began to pour in to support Tuskegee and other programs Washington had begun. Senators, governors, and presidents sought his advice. He soon became the spokesman for African Americans and the most powerful black man in America.

Washington's autobiography, *Up from Slavery*, published in 1901, further developed his views. When he died in 1915, he was still one of the most influential African Americans in the country.

From *The Souls of Black Folks,*
"Of Mr. Booker T. Washington and Others" ★ 1903

W.E.B. DuBOIS

1868–1963

W.E.B. DuBois championed the second major approach to achieving first-class citizenship for African Americans. He felt that African Americans should not accept racism, discrimination, or the violence that accompanied them. He advocated that African Americans fight for their rights as citizens, especially the right to vote. They were just as equal as whites, he thought, and should struggle to achieve equality. DuBois also believed that an educated African-American elite he called the Talented Tenth should lead that struggle for equality. W.E.B. DuBois became a founding member of the National Association for the Advancement of Colored People, one of the nation's foremost civil rights organizations. A leader in the word peace movement, DuBois also believed that African countries should play a major role in determining the future of the world.

asily the most striking thing in history of the American Negro since 1876 is the ascendancy of Mr. Booker T. Washington. It began at the time when war memories and ideals were rapidly passing; a day of astonishing commercial development was dawning; a sense of doubt and hesitation overtook the freedmen's sons—then it was that his leading began. Mr. Washington came, with a simple definite program, at the psychological moment when the nation was a little ashamed of having bestowed so much sentiment on Negroes, and was concentrating its energies on dollars. His program of industrial education, conciliation of the South, and submission and silence as to civil and political rights, was not wholly original; the free Negroes from 1830 up to wartime had striven to build industrial schools, and the American Missionary Association had from the first taught various trades; and Price [a civil rights leader] and others had sought a way of honorable alliance with the best of the Southerners. But Mr. Washington first indissolubly linked these things; he put enthusiasm, unlimited energy, and perfect faith into this program, and changed it from a bypath into a veritable way of life. And the tale of the methods by which he did this is a fascinating study of human life.

It startled the nation to hear a Negro advocating such a

program after many decades of bitter complaint; it startled and won the applause of the South, it interested and won the admiration of the North; and after a confused murmur of protest, it silenced if it did not convert the Negroes themselves.

To gain the sympathy and cooperation of the various elements comprising the white South was Mr. Washington's first task; and this, at the time Tuskegee was founded, seemed, for a black man, well-nigh impossible. And yet ten years later it was done in the word spoken at Atlanta: "In all things purely social we can be as separate as the five fingers, and yet one as the hand in all things essential to mutual progress." This "Atlanta Compromise" is by all odds the most notable thing in Mr. Washington's career. The South interpreted it in different ways: the radicals received it as a complete surrender of the demand for civil and political equality; the conservatives, as a generously conceived working basis for mutual understanding. So both approved it, and today its author is certainly the most distinguished Southerner since Jefferson Davis [President of the Confederacy], and the one with the largest personal following.

Next to this achievement comes Mr. Washington's work in gaining place and consideration in the North. Others less shrewd and tactful had formerly essayed to sit on these two stools and had fallen between them; but as Mr.

**"THE PROBLEM OF THE TWENTIETH CENTURY IS THE PROBLEM OF THE COLOR LINE."
—W.E.B. DuBois**

Washington knew the heart of the South from birth and training, so by singular insight he intuitively grasped the spirit of the age which was dominating the North. And so thoroughly did he learn the speech and thought of triumphant commercialism, and the ideals of material prosperity, that the picture of a lone black boy poring over French grammar amid the weeds and dirt of a neglected home soon seemed to him the acme of absurdities. One wonders what Socrates and St. Francis of Assisi would say to this.

And yet this very singleness of vision and thorough oneness with his age is a mark of the successful man. It is as though nature must needs make men narrow in order to give them force. So Mr. Washington's cult has gained unquestioning followers, his work has wonderfully prospered, his friends are legion, and his enemies are confounded. Today he stands as the one recognized spokesman of his ten million fellows, and one of the most notable figures in a nation of seventy millions. One hesitates, therefore, to criticize a life, which, beginning with so little, has done so much. And yet the time is come when one may speak in all sincerity and utter courtesy of the mistakes and shortcomings of Mr. Washington's career, as well as of his triumphs, without being thought captious or envious, and without forgetting that it is easier to do ill than well in the world ⋆

THE AUTHOR

An educator, writer, and social scientist, W.E.B. DuBois was one of the most significant African-American leaders of his time. When he earned his doctorate degree from Harvard University in 1895, he became the first African American to achieve that honor.

In 1909 DuBois helped to found the National Association for the Advancement of Colored People. From 1910 to 1934, he was the editor of *The Crisis*, a magazine published by the civil rights organization. *The Crisis* was a must-read for those interested in issues concerning African Americans. DuBois authored nineteen books and wrote numerous articles for magazines and newspapers during his long career. During his later years he moved to Ghana, Africa, where he died in 1963.

THE RESPONSE

In the beginning, DuBois shared some of Washington's views. Like Washington, he believed in self-help, racial solidarity, and economic cooperation. But as DuBois became more outspoken about racial injustice, he began to differ greatly with Washington. DuBois also felt that the enormous influence that Washington had was not good for African Americans.

With the essay in *The Souls of Black Folks*, DuBois expressed what many other African Americans felt about Booker T. Washington and his policies. They respected what the black leader had been able to accomplish in the area of education. Some also applauded Washington's efforts to establish black-owned businesses and his call to build up African-American communities. They did not, however, accept Washington's view that African Americans should accept second-class status and the violence and abuse that they faced daily. DuBois became the leader of this group.

"This country can have no more democracy than it accords and guarantees to the humblest and weakest citizen."

—James Weldon Johnson

"Lift Ev'ry Voice and Sing" ★ 1900

JAMES WELDON 1871–1938 JOHNSON

J. ROSAMOND 1873–1954 JOHNSON

The year was 1900. James Weldon Johnson had worked very hard to finish the lyrics to a song he was writing to help his school celebrate Abraham Lincoln's birthday. He wanted students at the Stanton School in Jacksonville, Florida, where he was principal, to sing the new song. His brother John Rosamond composed the music. The new song was "Lift Ev'ry Voice and Sing." Everyone at the Stanton School was moved by how the words expressed the pain and hope of African Americans.

Although the Johnson brothers would write more than two hundred songs together, "Lift Ev'ry Voice and Sing" would be their most famous. It is called the "Negro National Anthem" and is still sung today at important African-American gatherings.

ift ev'ry voice and sing,
Till earth and heaven ring,
Ring with the harmonies of Liberty;
Let our rejoicing rise
High as the list'ning skies,
Let it resound loud as the rolling sea.
Sing a song full of the faith that the dark past has taught us
Sing a song full of the hope that the present has brought us
Facing the rising sun of our new day begun,
Let us march on till victory is won.

Stony the road we trod,
Bitter the chast'ning rod,
Felt in the days when hope unborn had died;
Yet with a steady beat,
Have not our weary feet
Come to the place for which our fathers sighed?
We have come over a way that with tears has been watered
We have come, treading our path thro' the blood of the
    slaughtered,
Out from the gloomy past, till now we stand at last
Where the white gleam of our bright star is cast.

God of our weary years,
God of our silent tears,
Thou who hast brought us thus far on the way;

Thou who has by Thy might,

Led us into the light,

Keep us forever in the path, we pray.

Lest our feet stray from the places, our God,
    where we met Thee,

Lest our hearts, drunk with the wine of the world,
    we forget Thee;

Shadowed beneath Thy hand, may we forever stand,

True to our God, true to our native land ⋆

THE AUTHORS

James Weldon Johnson was born in Jacksonville, Florida. A songwriter, poet, journalist, novelist, educator, and civil rights activist, he became one of black America's most influential leaders. Some of his published work is still popular, including *God's Trombones: Seven Negro Sermons in Verse* and *Autobiography of an Ex-Colored Man*. He served as executive secretary of the National Association for the Advancement of Colored People from 1920 until 1931 and helped to establish it as a major civil rights organization.

After attending the New England Conservatory of Music, John Rosamond Johnson pursued a career as a Broadway composer. He; his brother, James; and Bob Cole wrote a number of musical revues for Broadway. John was also an actor. The first African American to conduct a white orchestra for a white cast in a New York theater, he later became musical director of the Grand Opera House in London, England.

THE RESPONSE

The Johnson brothers sent "Lift Ev'ry Voice and Sing" to their New York publisher and forgot about it. But the schoolchildren remembered the song and passed it on to other children. Soon "Lift Ev'ry Voice and Sing" was being sung at African-American schools throughout the South. Church choirs began to sing it. Then the NAACP adopted it as the "Negro National Anthem." In less than twenty years what had been written for a school presentation had become the most popular and respected song among African Americans.

From a Speech Delivered at Liberty Hall, New York City ⋆ NOVEMBER 25, 1922

MARCUS GARVEY

1887–1940

Black nationalism is a movement among African Americans that emphasizes their African origin, their pride in being black, and the desire to control their own communities. It sometimes includes the desire to establish a black nation in Africa or in some part of the United States.

A call for black nationalism has been a part of the African-American struggle for freedom since the 1700s. In the early 1800s, Paul Cuffe, an African-American sea captain, transported a number of black people to Africa. Other prominent black nationalists included David Walker, Martin Delany, and W.E.B. DuBois. The first black nationalist mass movement in the United States took place in the early 1900s. It was led by Marcus Garvey, who recruited thousands to his Universal Negro Improvement Association (UNIA).

e shall march out, yes, as black American citizens, as black British subjects, as black French citizens, as black Italians or as black Spaniards, but we shall march out with greater loyalty, the loyalty of race. We shall march out in answer to the cry of our fathers, who cry out to us for the redemption of our own country, our motherland, Africa.

We shall march out, not forgetting the blessings of America. We shall march out, not forgetting the blessings of civilization. We shall march out with the history of peace before and behind us, and surely that history shall be our breastplate, for how can man fight better than knowing that the cause for which he fights is righteous? How can man fight more gloriously than by knowing that behind him is a history of slavery, a history of bloody carnage and massacre inflicted upon a race because of its inability to protect itself and fight? Shall we not fight for the glorious opportunity of protecting and forever more establishing ourselves as a mighty race and nation, never more to be disrespected by men. Glorious shall be the battle when the time comes to fight for our people and our race.

"TEACH YOUR CHILDREN THEY ARE DIRECT DECENDANTS OF THE GREATEST AND PROUDEST RACE WHO EVER PEOPLED THE EARTH."
—Marcus Garvey

We should say to the millions who are in Africa to hold the fort, for we are coming, four hundred million strong ★

THE AUTHOR

Marcus Garvey was born in Jamaica. After leaving school at age fourteen, he worked as a printer and joined several Jamaican nationalist organizations. In 1916 he moved to the United States during a period of political and cultural awakening. In 1917 Garvey established a United States branch of the Universal Negro Improvement Association, an organization he had formed in Jamaica. By the early 1920s, UNIA had hundreds of chapters worldwide and nearly a million members. In 1923 Garvey was convicted of using the U.S. mail to defraud his followers. He served three years in prison, and was deported to Jamaica. He never returned to the United States.

THE RESPONSE

Thousands of blacks responded to Garvey's call for economic independence, racial pride, and the need for African Americans to return to Africa. Black-owned restaurants, grocery stores, hotels, a weekly newspaper, and a steamship line were established. For the first time, many African Americans felt a sense of pride about their African heritage. Within a few short years, UNIA had become the coordinator of the largest organized mass movement in African-American history. It paved the way for other nationalist movements, such as the Nation of Islam.

"The whole world opened to me when I learned to read."

—*Mary McLeod Bethune*

From "Faith That Moved a Dump Heap" ★ JUNE 1941

MARY McLEOD BETHUNE

1875–1955

In 1787 the first public school for African Americans, the African Free School, opened in New York City. For the most part, however, schools for African Americans were housed in churches and homes of African-American leaders. Some abolitionists also opened schools. After the Civil War, church groups opened many schools in the South for newly freed slaves. And during Reconstruction, governments established schools. But African Americans continued to take the lead in helping to educate their people, especially after Reconstruction ended. School systems run by whites often refused to provide money or give sufficient funding to educate African Americans. Dedicated African Americans such as Booker T. Washington, Charlotte Hawkins Brown, and Mary McLeod Bethune established their own institutions to provide educational opportunities for African Americans. These tireless educators help put education at the forefront of the African-American agenda.

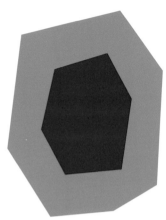

n October 3, 1904, I opened the doors of my school, with an enrollment of five little girls . . . whose parents paid me fifty cents' weekly tuition. . . . I considered cash money as the smallest part of my resources. I had faith in a living God, faith in myself, and a desire to serve. . . .

We burned logs and used the charred splinters as pencils, and mashed elderberries for ink. I begged strangers for a broom, a lamp, a bit of cretonne to put around the packing case which served as my desk. I haunted the city dump and the trash piles behind hotels, retrieving discarded linen and kitchenware, cracked dishes, broken chairs, pieces of old lumber. Everything was scoured and mended. This was part of the training to salvage, to reconstruct, to make bricks without straw. As parents began gradually to leave their children overnight, I had to provide sleeping accommodations. . . .

The school expanded fast. In less than two years I had 250 pupils. In desperation I hired a large hall next to my original little cottage, and used it as a combined dormitory and classroom. I concentrated more and more on girls, as I felt that they especially were hampered by lack of educational opportunities. . . .

I had many volunteer workers and few regular teachers, who were paid from fifteen to twenty-five dollars a month and board. I was supposed to keep the balance of the funds for my own pocket, but there was never any balance—only a yawning hole. I wore old clothes sent me by mission boards, recut and redesigned for me in our dress-making classes. At last I saw that our only solution was to stop renting space, and to buy and build our own college.

Near by was a field, popularly called Hells' Hole, which was used as a dumping ground. I approached the owner, determined to buy it. The price was $250. In a daze, he finally agreed to take five dollars down, and the balance in two years. I promised to be back in a few days with the initial payment. He never knew it, but I didn't have five dollars. I raised this sum selling ice cream and sweet-potato pies to the workmen on construction jobs, and I took the owner his money in small change wrapped in my handkerchief.

That's how the Bethune-Cookman college campus started ⋆

THE AUTHOR

Mary McLeod Bethune was an educator, civil rights leader, and founder of both the Bethune-Cookman College in Florida and the National Council of Negro Women. She was also an adviser to presidents and was the first African-American woman appointed to a federal administrative position. Born in Mayesville, South Carolina, Bethune became one of the most influential African Americans in the United States.

THE RESPONSE

Mary McLeod Bethune established one of the finest institutions for African-American girls, the Daytona Normal and Industrial Institute for Negro Girls. In 1923, it merged with another African-American school, resulting in Bethune-Cookman College, a leading, predominately black institution. Bethune remained as its president. During her career, Bethune championed the cause of education for African Americans. She secured scholarships and made education a possibility for thousands.

"The Negro Speaks of Rivers" ★ 1921

LANGSTON HUGHES

1902–1967

The Harlem Renaissance was a period of great cultural and artistic accomplishment by African Americans. During this period of the 1920s and 1930s, many African Americans produced great works of literature, art, and music. And much of what these artists, writers, and musicians produced focused on black pride and black cultural heritage. Harlem, located in New York City, was the primary meeting place for the artists. Most of them visited Harlem, and many lived there during the height of the Renaissance. Some of the leading figures during this period included James Weldon Johnson, Claude McKay, Countee Cullen, Alain Locke, and Jean Toomer. Langston Hughes, one of America's most prolific writers, was a major participant in the Renaissance.

I've known rivers:

I've known rivers ancient as the world and older
than the flow of human blood in human veins.

My soul has grown deep like the rivers.

I bathed in the Euphrates when dawns were young.
I built my hut near the Congo and it lulled me to sleep.
I looked upon the Nile and raised the pyramids above it.
I heard the singing of the Mississippi when Abe Lincoln went
down to New Orleans, and I've seen its muddy bosom turn
all golden in the sunset.

I've known rivers:
Ancient, dusky rivers.

My soul has grown deep like the rivers ★

*"THERE ARE
MANY BARRIERS
PEOPLE TRY TO
BREAK DOWN.
I TRY TO DO IT
WITH POETRY."*
—Langston Hughes

THE AUTHOR

Langston Hughes was born in Joplin, Missouri. He began writing at an early age, serving as class poet and editor of his high school yearbook. He attended Columbia University in New York and graduated from Lincoln University, a historically black college in Pennsylvania. Hughes's work focuses on African-American life. During a long, distinguished career, he wrote poetry, plays, novels, lyrics, magazine articles, and children's books. He also edited anthologies that gave other African-American writers an opportunity to be published. Hughes won numerous awards, and is considered a leading writer of the twentieth century.

THE RESPONSE

Langston Hughes wrote "The Negro Speaks of Rivers" while visiting his father, who had moved to Mexico. Published in *The Crisis* magazine, this poem launched Langston Hughes's writing career. Other poems were published in *The Crisis*. In 1925 *Opportunity* magazine awarded Hughes first prize in its literary contest for the poem "The Weary Blues." This recognition helped him land a book contract, and in 1926 he published his first collection of verse, entitled *The Weary Blues.* Langston Hughes was one of the most celebrated writers of the Harlem Renaissance. His body of work, which continued into the 1960s, earned him the title "Poet Laureate of the Negro Race."

From *Their Eyes Were Watching God* ★ **1937**

ZORA NEALE HURSTON

1901–1960

Sometimes the work of writers achieves greater success decades after it is first published. That is the case with Zora Neale Hurston. Her career as a writer began during the Harlem Renaissance in the 1930s. And in the two decades that followed, she became one of the country's most noted African-American writers. But after the publication of her last book, *Seraph on the Suwanee* in 1948, Hurston disappeared from the literary scene. She worked as a substitute teacher, librarian, and maid. In 1960, she died in poverty and obscurity in the St. Lucie County Welfare Home in Florida.

Beginning in the 1970s, there was renewed interest in Hurston's work. Her books, published in the 1930s and 1940s, are extremely popular today—more so than when they were first released.

here was a finished silence after that so that for the first time they could hear the wind picking at the pine trees. It made Pheoby think of Sam waiting for her and getting fretful. It made Janie think about that room upstairs—her bedroom. Pheoby hugged Janie real hard and cut the darkness in flight.

Soon everything around downstairs was shut and fastened. Janie mounted the stairs with her lamp. The light in her hand was like a spark of sun-stuff washing her face in fire. Her shadow behind fell back and headlong down the stairs. Now, in her room, the place tasted fresh again. The wind through the open windows had broomed out all the fetid feeling of absence and nothingness. She closed in and sat down. Combing road-dust out of her hair. Thinking.

The day of the gun, and the bloody body, and the courthouse came and commenced to sing a sobbing sigh out of every corner of the room; out of each and every chair and thing. Commenced to sing, commenced to sob and sigh, singing and sobbing. Then Tea Cake came prancing around her where she was and the song of the sigh flew out of the window and lit in the top of the pine trees. Tea Cake, with the sun for a shawl. Of course he wasn't dead. He could never be dead until she herself had finished feeling and thinking. The kiss of his memory made pictures of love

"LEARNING WITHOUT WISDOM IS A LOAD OF BOOKS ON A DONKEY'S BACK."
—Zora Neale Hurston

and light against the wall. Here was peace. She pulled in her horizon like a great fish-net. Pulled it from around the waist of the world and draped it over her shoulder. So much of life in its meshes! She called in her soul to come and see ★

THE AUTHOR

Zora Neale Hurston was born and raised in Eatonville, an all-black town in Florida. She received her bachelor's degree from Barnard College and a graduate degree from Columbia University, where she studied anthropology and African-American folktales.

Hurston is best known for her books about African-American life, African-American folktales, and women's independence. Her short stories first appeared in *Opportunity* magazine. Her first book, *Jonah's Gourd Vine*, was published in 1934. She published ten books between 1934 and 1948. Hurston died in obscurity and poverty in 1960.

THE RESPONSE

Author Alice Walker has helped to bring renewed attention to Zora Neale Hurston's work. In 1973 Walker found Hurston's unmarked grave in Ft. Pierce, Florida, and had a tombstone erected there. On the tombstone she had inscribed, ZORA NEALE HURSTON, A GENIUS OF THE SOUTH, 1901–1960, NOVELIST, FOLKLORIST, ANTHROPOLOGIST.

Hurston's work, especially *Their Eyes Were Watching God*, is used in women's and African-American literature classes across the nation. Every January the Zora Neale Hurston Festival of the Arts and Humanities, held in her hometown of Eatonville, Florida, draws more than 100,000 people. The Zora Neale Hurston Museum of Fine Arts and the Zora Neale Hurston Youth Institute are also located in Eatonville.

"Take my hand,
precious lord,
Lead me home."

—*Thomas A. Dorsey*

"Take My Hand, Precious Lord" ★ 1938

THOMAS A. DORSEY

1901–1960

Today, gospel music is an important part of African-American church services. This music, which combines elements of spirituals, hymns, blues, and the African musical tradition, emerged in the early 1900s. Gospel music offers an opportunity for praise and joyous worship of God through music.

One of the pioneers of this music was Reverend Charles A. Tindley, a Methodist Episcopalian minister from Philadelphia. Tindley wrote more than forty hymns that drew from the African-American music tradition rather than copying the European hymn style. Thomas A. Dorsey, however, a former blues and jazz performer, is called the "Father of Gospel Music." He brought the blues influence to his gospel songs and helped to popularize the music by taking it to all parts of the country.

Precious Lord, take my hand,
Lead me on, let me stand,
I am tired, I am weak, I am worn;
Thru the storm, thru the night,
Lead me on to the light,
Take my hand, precious Lord, Lead me home.

When my way grows drear,
precious Lord, linger near,
When my life is almost gone,
Hear my cry, hear my call,
Hold my hand lest I fall;
Take my hand, precious Lord, Lead me home.

When the darkness appears
and the night draws near,
And the day is past and gone,
At the river I stand,
Guide my feet, hold my hand;
Take my hand, precious Lord, Lead me home. ★

THE AUTHOR

Thomas A. Dorsey was the son of a minister. He learned how to play the piano when he was very young. Dorsey began his musical career playing piano in nightclubs and for the legendary blues singer Ma Rainey. He went on to write hundreds of blues and jazz songs. Beginning in 1929, he focused exclusively on religious music. He wrote songs, headed his own publishing company, directed choirs, lectured, and taught his new style of music. He helped to develop some of gospel music's most celebrated singers. Dorsey has had greater impact on African-American church music than perhaps any other composer.

THE RESPONSE

This new church music was not quickly accepted by traditional African-American churchgoers. They had grown accustomed to the spirituals and hymns that had been sung in their churches. Because of its blues influence, many of them viewed Dorsey's music as the devil's music. During the 1930s gospel was centered in Chicago where Dorsey lived. But by the 1940s it had been accepted on a national scale. Songs recorded by gospel groups and tours by Thomas A. Dorsey helped to expose his music to a wider audience.

Gospel music has had a tremendous influence on many areas of popular music, including country, rock, and rhythm and blues. A large number of leading African-American singers and musicians got their start in gospel music, including Aretha Franklin, Sam Cooke, Ray Charles, Lou Rawls, and Mavis Staples.

From *Native Son* ★ 1940

RICHARD WRIGHT

1901–1960

Richard Wright's career as a writer began after the Harlem Renaissance ended. But his achievements would earn him recognition as the father of the modern African-American novel. *Native Son*, a novel he published in 1940, became a landmark in American and African-American literature. Its brutally honest portrayal of racism, poverty, and injustice shocked America as no other book about African-American life had.

Wright had a major impact on almost all African-American novelists published after World War II. His realistic and naturalistic approach influenced writers such as Ralph Ellison, James Baldwin, Chester Himes, and Ann Petry.

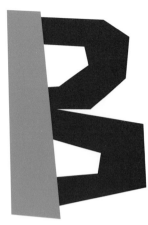*rrrrrrriiiiiiiiiiiiiiiiiiiinng!*

An alarm clock clanged in the dark and silent room. A bed spring creaked. A woman's voice sang out impatiently:

"Bigger, shut that thing off!"

A surly grunt sounded above the tinny ring of metal. Naked feet swished dryly across the planks in the wooden floor and the clang ceased abruptly.

"Turn on the light, Bigger."

"Awright," came a sleepy mumble.

Light flooded the room and revealed a black boy standing in a narrow space between two iron beds, rubbing his eyes with the backs of his hands. From a bed to his right the woman spoke again:

"Buddy, get up from there! I got a big washing on my hands today and I want you-all out of here."

Another black boy rolled from the bed and stood up. The woman also rose and stood in her nightgown.

"Turn your heads so I can dress," she said.

The two boys averted their eyes and gazed into a far corner of the room. The woman rushed out of her nightgown and put on a pair of step-ins. She turned to the bed from which she had risen and called:

"Vera! Get up from there!"

"What time is it, Ma?" asked a muffled, adolescent voice from beneath a quilt.

"Get up from there, I say!"

"O.K., Ma."

A brown-skinned girl in a cotton gown got up and stretched her arms above her head and yawned. Sleepily, she sat on a chair and fumbled with her stockings. The two boys kept their faces averted while their mother and sister put on enough clothes to keep them from feeling ashamed; and the mother and sister did the same while the boys dressed. Abruptly, they all paused, holding their clothes in their hands, their attention caught by a light tapping in the thinly plastered walls of the room. They forgot their conspiracy against shame and their eyes strayed apprehensively over the floor.

"There he is again, Bigger!" the woman screamed, and the tiny, one-room apartment galvanized into violent action. A chair toppled as the woman, half-dressed and in her stocking feet, scrambled breathlessly upon the bed. Her two sons, barefoot, stood tense and motionless, their eyes searching anxiously under the bed and chairs. The girl ran into a corner, half-stooped and gathered the hem of her slip into both of her hands and held it tightly over her knees.

"Oh! Oh!" she wailed.

"There he goes!"

The woman pointed a shaking finger. Her eyes were round with fascinated horror.

"Where?"

"I don't see 'im!"

"I DO NOT DEAL IN HAPPINESS. I DEAL IN MEANING."
—Richard Wright

"Bigger, he's behind the trunk!" the girl whimpered.

"Vera!" the woman screamed. "Get up here on the bed. Don't let that thing bite you!"

Frantically, Vera climbed upon the bed and the woman caught hold of her. With their arms entwined about each other, the black mother and the brown daughter gazed open-mouthed at the trunk in the corner.

Bigger looked around the room wildly, then darted to a curtain and swept it aside and grabbed two heavy iron skillets from a wall above a gas stove. He whirled and called softly to his brother, his eyes glued to the trunk.

"Buddy!"

"Yeah?"

"Here; take this skillet."

"O.K."

"Now, get over by the door!"

"O.K."

Buddy crouched by the door and held the iron skillet by its handle, his arm flexed and poised. Save for the quick, deep breathing of the four people, the room was quiet. Bigger crept on tiptoe toward the trunk with the skillet clutched stiffly in his hand, his eyes dancing and watching every inch of the wooden floor in front of him. He paused and, without moving an eye or muscle, called:

"Buddy!"

"Hunh?"

"Put that box in front of the hole so he can't get out!"

Buddy ran to a wooden box and shoved it quickly in front of a gaping hole in the molding and then backed again to the door, holding the skillet ready. Bigger eased to the trunk and peered behind it cautiously. He saw nothing. Carefully, he stuck out his bare foot and pushed the trunk a few inches.

"There he is!" the mother screamed again.

A huge black rat squealed and leaped at Bigger's trouser-leg and snagged it in his teeth, hanging on ⋆

THE AUTHOR

Richard Wright was born near Natchez, Mississippi. After a difficult childhood, he moved to Chicago when he was nineteen, taking his love of reading with him. He began writing seriously after arriving in Chicago. Some of his essays and short stories were published in magazines. His first book, *Uncle Tom's Children*, was published in 1938 after he moved to New York. It was well received, but his second book, *Native Son*, published in 1940, was an enormous success. Following the publication of his autobiography, *Black Boy*, Wright moved to Paris, France, where he continued to write. He died in Paris of a heart attack.

THE RESPONSE

Native Son was the first African-American novel to receive both critical and commercial success. Within three weeks of its release, 200,000 copies were sold. It was the first book written by an African American to become a Book-of-the-Month Club selection. It was adapted to the stage and a film version was produced. *Native Son* is still extremely popular today. Although written more than sixty years ago, many readers can still relate to Wright's story of urban ghetto life, racism, and poverty.

"Freedom is
a precious
thing,
and the inalienable
birthright of all
who travel this earth."

—Paul Robeson

From an Address at a Public Meeting Sponsored by the Council of African Affairs, Madison Square Garden, New York City ⋆ **JUNE 6, 1946**

PAUL ROBESON

1898–1976

During the 1930s and 1940s, no African American was more popular than Paul Robeson. He was a brilliant stage actor and concert singer, as well as a movie actor. Robeson spoke several different languages, was a scholar, and had been a college football All-American. Some considered the multitalented African American to be one of the most distinguished men in America. But when Robeson began to speak out against racism and lynching in the United States, and oppression abroad, he became one of the most vilified men in America. The government accused him of being a Communist and took away his passport. Concert promoters in the United States refused to book him. Paul Robeson paid a very high price for daring to speak out against racism and injustice.

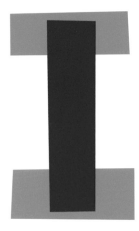I have spoken for other causes on other occasions in this great hall. And while they were all important causes about which I was keenly concerned, I think I can say that never before have I faced such an audience as this with the sense of responsibility, of urgency, of intimacy with you that I now feel.

The Negro—and I mean American Negroes as well as West Indians and Africans—has a direct and firsthand understanding, which most other people lack, of what imperialist exploitation and oppression is. With him it is no far-off theoretical problem. In his daily life he experiences the same system of job discrimination, segregation and denial of democratic rights whereby the imperialist overlords keep hundreds of millions of people in colonial subjection throughout the world.

The one basic difference is that here in America the Negro has the law—at least partially, and in some sections of the country—on his side, and he has powerful allies in the ranks of white organized labor directly involved in his daily fight for justice. In Africa, in the West Indies, and in Asia, the colonial peoples wage a desperate struggle for recognition simply as human beings—as human beings to whom human rights are due. And these colonial peoples fight alone in each country—alone except for the help which reaches them from afar, from world-conscious labor in free countries and from other anti-fascist, anti-imperialist forces.

And that is why we are gathered here tonight. Because our own rights and liberties—even though limited—are far, far greater than those of our brothers in colonial bondage. Because we must exercise the greater strength which we have to help win freedom for them. And also because in that very process of helping others, we add to our own strength and bring nearer full freedom for ourselves ⋆

THE AUTHOR

Paul Robeson was born in Princeton, New Jersey. He attended Rutgers University on a scholarship and was an outstanding athlete. He also achieved Phi Beta Kappa honors. While earning his law degree from Columbia University, he was seen in an amateur theatrical production by playwright Eugene O'Neill. O'Neill cast him in his play *The Emperor Jones* and Robeson's stage career was launched. In 1925 he made his concert debut. For the next several decades Paul Robeson starred on Broadway and in movies and performed in concert.

THE RESPONSE

In the 1940s Paul Robeson began to speak out more about racism and oppression. He expressed his concerns in countries such as Russia, England, France, and India as well as in the United States. The United States government soon branded him a threat to the country and began to crack down on him. Concert promoters and record companies shunned him. He was banned from television. When his passport was taken from him in 1950, he was not able to leave the country to pursue his career. Robeson is now remembered as a champion in the struggle for civil rights and human dignity. He was the first African-American superstar.

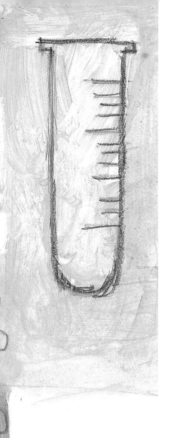

From *The Man Who Talked with Flowers* · 1939

GEORGE WASHINGTON CARVER

1861(?)–1943

African-American slaves could not get patents for their inventions because slaves were considered property and not citizens. Even those African Americans who were free found it difficult to secure credit and protection for their creations. Most inventions by African Americans were credited to whites. After the Civil War, some African Americans began to secure patents. Jan Matzelinger, William Purvis, Elijah McCoy, Andrew Beard, Granville T. Woods, and Lewis Latimer are a few of those who received patents for very important inventions. George Washington Carver, a scientist, was one of the most important inventors of the early 1900s.

Although he had many inventions to his credit, Carver was only issued three patents. He freely gave his discoveries to benefit humankind. "God gave them to me. How can I sell them to someone else?" he once asked. The following poem expresses the spiritual side of this dedicated man.

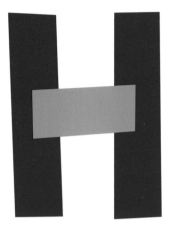 ow do I talk to the flower?

Through it I walk to the Infinite.

And what is the infinite?

It is that silent, small force.

It isn't the outer physical contact. No, it isn't that.

The infinite is not confirmed in the visible world.

It is not in the earthquake, the wind or the fire.

It is that still small voice that calls up the fairies.

Yet when you look out upon God's beautiful world—there it is.

When you look into the heart of a rose there you experience
it—but you can't explain it.

There are certain things, often very little things, like the little
peanut, the little piece of clay, the little flower that cause you
to look WITHIN—

and then it is that you see the soul of things ⋆

**"EDUCATION IS
THE KEY TO
UNLOCK THE
GOLDEN DOOR
OF FREEDOM."**
**—George
Washington
Carver**

THE AUTHOR

George Washington Carver was born in Missouri during the Civil War. In 1889 he enrolled at Simpson College in Iowa. At first he wanted to be an artist, but his love of nature led him to study horticulture. He received a master's degree from Simpson. In 1896 Booker T. Washington invited him to head the newly formed agriculture department at Tuskegee Institute. Carver did his research there until his death in 1943.

Carver was a simple man who did not like the spotlight. This tireless researcher helped to revolutionize agriculture in the South. He introduced the basics of soil enrichment, which helped the land become more productive. He introduced new crops, such as sweet potatoes and peanuts, that grew well in Southern soil. He also developed more than four hundred products from them. His fame as a scientist grew, and he was recognized as the man who helped to rescue the Southern economy.

THE RESPONSE

Among the many contributions made by George Washington Carver was a crop-rotation method he developed at Tuskegee Institute. It introduced new crops such as sweet potatoes, peanuts, and soybeans that helped revitalize the farmland of the South. He then invented hundreds of new products from the new crops. His efforts helped stimulate a struggling Southern agricultural economy. Carver became a hero in the South and one of America's most honored scientists. The Royal Society of Arts in London, England, made him an honorary member. In 1923, the National Association for the Advancement of Colored People presented him with the prestigious Spingarn Medal for his contributions to agriculture. Honorary degrees were bestowed upon him. On July 14, 1943, six months after his death, President Franklin D. Roosevelt designated Washington's boyhood home in Diamond, Missouri, a national monument.

"The only way to get equality is for two people to get the same thing at the same time at the same place."

—*Thurgood Marshall*

From the Summary of Argument, *Brown* v. *Board of Education of Topeka, Kansas* ★ OCTOBER, 1953

THURGOOD MARSHALL

1908–1993

In 1896, in the *Plessy* v. *Ferguson* case, the United States Supreme Court ruled that segregation was permissible as long as equal facilities were provided for both races. This decision supported a doctrine called "separate but equal," which was employed in all aspects of public life.

During the first half of the twentieth century, America was still very much segregated. African Americans couldn't stay in hotels frequented by whites, they couldn't eat in the same restaurants as whites. Their children couldn't go to the same schools that white children attended. There were basically two different Americas: one black and the other white. Segregation is the word used to describe this system. Many people had been fighting for years to change "Jim Crow" laws that supported segregation. The National Association for the Advancement of Colored People (NAACP) and others fought against these laws in court. A few local and state cases were won. But in 1954, in a case brought before the United States Supreme Court, the NAACP won an enormous victory. In *Brown* v. *Board of Education of Topeka, Kansas*, the Supreme Court ruled that separate facilities were unequal and that racial segregation violates the equal protection clause of the Fourteenth Amendment. Legalized segregation in America had been struck a fatal blow.

These cases consolidated for argument before this Court present in different factual contexts essentially the same ultimate legal questions.

The substantive question common to all is whether a state can, consistently with the Constitution, exclude children, solely on the ground that they are Negroes, from public schools which otherwise they would be qualified to attend. It is the thesis of this brief, submitted on behalf of the excluded children, that the answer to the question is in the negative: the Fourteenth Amendment prevents states from according differential treatment to American children on the basis of their color or race. Both the legal precedents and the judicial theories, discussed in Part I hereof, and the evidence concerning the intent of the framers of the Fourteenth Amendment and the understanding of the Congress and the ratifying states, developed in Part II hereof, support this proposition.

Denying this thesis, the school authorities, relying in part on language originating in this Court's opinion in *Plessy* v. *Ferguson*, 163 U.S. 537, urge that exclusion of Negroes, qua Negroes, from designated public schools is permissible when the excluded children are afforded admittance to other schools especially reserved for Negroes, *qua* Negroes, if such schools are equal.

The procedural question common to all the cases is the

role to be played, and the time-table to be followed, by this Court and the lower courts in directing an end to the challenged exclusion, in the event that this Court determines, with respect to the substantive question, that exclusion of Negroes, *qua* Negroes, from public schools contravenes the Constitution.

The importance to our American democracy of the substantive question can hardly be overstated. The question is whether a nation founded on the proposition that "all men are created equal" is honoring its commitments to grant "due process of law" and "the equal protection of the laws" to all within its borders when it, or one of its constituent states, confers or denies benefits on the basis of color or race ★

THE AUTHOR

Thurgood Marshall was born in Baltimore, Maryland. He graduated from Lincoln University and received his law degree from Howard University in 1933. After several years in private practice, he began a long career with the NAACP. He was responsible for handling all cases involving African-American constitutional rights. Marshall argued thirty-two cases before the U.S. Supreme Court and won twenty-nine of them. In 1967, he became the first African American to serve on the United States Supreme Court.

THE RESPONSE

The case *Brown* v. *Board of Education of Topeka, Kansas* is one of the most important cases in the history of the United States Supreme Court. It dealt legal segregation in public places, including schools, a death blow. But enforcing the new law of the land would prove to be a long and difficult struggle. A main thrust of the civil rights movement of the 1950s and 1960s was to force state and local governments to honor the new law. The decision in *Brown* v. *Board of Education of Topeka, Kansas* influenced major civil rights legislation such as the Voting Rights Act and the Civil Rights acts of the 1960s.

"I was determined
to achieve the total
freedom that our
history lessons
taught us we were entitled to,
no matter what
the sacrifice."

—*Rosa Parks*

From *Rosa Parks: My Story* ★ 1992

ROSA PARKS

1913–

About a year and a half after the *Brown* v. *Board of Education of Topeka, Kansas* decision was rendered, another major event in the civil rights struggle took place. In Montgomery, Alabama, in 1955, a small but determined woman refused to give up her seat on a bus to a white man. She was tired of being pushed around and forced to accept horrible indignities because of her color. Forced from the bus, Rosa Parks was booked at the police station and charged with disorderly conduct. Her act of courage, however, gave birth to the Montgomery bus boycott. It helped set the stage for Dr. Martin Luther King, Jr., and it helped to usher in a new thrust in the African-American struggle for justice and equality.

hen I got off from work that evening of December 1, I went to Court Square as usual to catch the Cleveland Avenue bus home. I didn't look to see who was driving when I got on, and by the time I recognized him, I had already paid my fare. It was the same driver who had put me off the bus back in 1943, twelve years earlier. He was still tall and heavy, with red, rough-looking skin. And he was still mean-looking. I didn't know if he had been on that route before—they switched the drivers around sometimes. I do know that most of the time if I saw him on a bus, I wouldn't get on it.

I saw a vacant seat in the middle section of the bus and took it. I didn't even question why there was a vacant seat even though there were quite a few people standing in the back. If I had thought about it at all, I would probably have figured maybe someone saw me get on and did not take the seat but left it vacant for me. There was a man sitting next to the window and two women across the aisle.

The next stop was the Empire Theater, and some whites got on. They filled up the white seats, and one man was left standing. The driver looked back and noticed the man standing. Then he looked back at us. He said, "Let me have those front seats," because they were the front seats of the black section. Didn't anybody move. We just sat right where we were, the four of us. Then he spoke a second time: "Y'all better make it light on yourselves and let me have those seats."

The man in the window seat next to me stood up, and I moved to let him pass by me, and then I looked across the aisle and saw that the two women were also standing. I moved over to the window seat. I could not see how standing up was going to "make it light" for me. The more we gave in and complied, the worse they treated us.

I thought back to the time I used to sit up all night and didn't sleep, and my grandfather would have his gun right by the fireplace, or if he had his one-horse wagon going anywhere, he always had his gun in the back of the wagon. People always say that I didn't give up my seat because I was tired, but that isn't true. I was not tired physically, or no more tired than I usually was at the end of a working day. I was not old, although some people have an image of me as being old then. I was forty-two. No, the only tired I was, was tired of giving in.

The driver of the bus saw me still sitting there, and he asked was I going stand up. I said, "No." He said, "Well, I'm going to have you arrested." Then I said, "You may do that." These were the only words we said to each other.

I didn't even know his name, which was James Blake, until we were in court together. He got out of the bus and stayed outside for a few minutes, waiting for the police.

As I sat there, I tried not to think about what might happen. I knew that anything was possible. I could be manhandled or beaten. I could be arrested. People have asked me if it occurred to me then that I could be the test case the NAACP had been looking for. I did not think about that at all. In fact if I had let myself think too deeply about what might happen to me, I might have gotten off the bus. But I chose to remain ★

THE AUTHOR

Rosa Parks was born in Tuskegee, Alabama, but grew up and made her home in Montgomery. She worked as a seamstress in a department store, and her husband, Raymond, was a barber.

Many people think Parks's refusal to give up her seat was her first act of protest. It was not. She was a member of the local NAACP chapter and served as its secretary. Following the successful boycott, Parks and her husband moved to Detroit, Michigan, where she worked for U.S. Representative John Conyers for a number of years.

THE RESPONSE

After Parks's arrest, members of the African-American community rallied behind her. They, too, had grown tired of the "Jim Crow" laws and the mistreatment by whites. They decided to stage a boycott of Montgomery buses. African Americans would not ride the buses in Montgomery until the city ended its segregated seating system. It was a yearlong struggle, but Montgomery officials finally agreed to end segregation on its buses. Dr. Martin Luther King, Jr., who had led the boycott, emerged as a national leader in the civil rights movement. He and other ministers from Montgomery formed the Southern Christian Leadership Conference, which would become a leading civil rights organization.

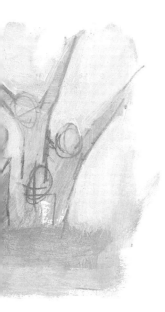

From a Speech Delivered at Lincoln University, Pennsylvania • JUNE 6, 1961

DR. MARTIN LUTHER KING, JR.

1929–1968

One of the most recognized names in American and world history is Dr. Martin Luther King, Jr. Although he lived for thirty-nine short years, his life's work had an enormous impact that is still felt today. His speeches are recited by thousands of schoolchildren across the country every year, including "I Have a Dream." A man committed to nonviolence, Dr. King spent his entire life in the fight for full citizenship for African Americans, and for rights for the poor and disadvantaged.

King believed in nonviolent civil disobedience, which he learned from studying the life and teachings of Mahatma Gandhi. This included using tactics such as marches, picketing, and boycotts to change repressive laws and conditions.

This speech, presented to African-American students at Lincoln University in Pennsylvania, one of the oldest historically black universities, was delivered two years before the famous "I Have a Dream" speech.

Today you bid farewell to the friendly security of this academic environment, a setting that will remain dear to you as long as the cords of memory shall lengthen. As you go out today to enter the clamorous highways of life, I should like to discuss with you some aspects of the American dream. For in a real sense, America is essentially a dream, a dream as yet unfulfilled. It is a dream of a land where men of all races, of all nationalities and of all creeds can live together as brothers. The substance of the dream is expressed in these sublime words, words lifted to cosmic proportions: "We hold these truths to be self-evident, that all men are created equal, that they are endowed by their Creator with certain unalienable rights, that among these are life, liberty, and the pursuit of happiness." This is the dream.

One of the first things we notice in this dream is an amazing universalism. It does not say some men, but it says all men. It does not say all white men, but it says all men, which includes black men. It does not say all Gentiles, but it says all men, which includes Jews. It does not say all Protestants, but it says all men, which includes Catholics.

And there is another thing we see in this dream that

ultimately distinguishes democracy and our form of government from all of the totalitarian regimes that emerge in history. It says that each individual has certain basic rights that are neither conferred by nor derived from the state. To discover where they came from it is necessary to move back behind the dim mist of eternity, for they are God-given. Very seldom if ever in the history of the world has a sociopolitical document expressed in such profoundly eloquent and unequivocal language the dignity and the worth of human personality. The American dream reminds us that every man is heir to the legacy of worthiness.

Ever since the founding fathers of our nation dreamed this noble dream, America has been something of a schizophrenic personality, tragically divided against herself. On the one hand we have proudly professed the principles of democracy, and on the other hand we have sadly practiced the very antithesis of those principles. Indeed slavery and segregation have been strange paradoxes in a nation founded on the principle that all men are created equal. This is what the Swedish sociologist, Gunnar Myrdal, referred to as the American dilemma.

But the shape of the world today does not permit us the luxury of an anemic democracy. The price America must pay for the continued exploitation of the Negro and other minority groups is the price of its own destruction. The hour is late; the clock of destiny is ticking out. It is trite, but

"IT MAY GET ME CRUCIFIED, I MAY EVEN DIE. BUT I WANT IT SAID EVEN IF I DIE IN THE STRUGGLE THAT 'HE DIED TO MAKE MEN FREE.'"
—Dr. Martin Luther King, Jr.

urgently true, that if America is to remain a first-class nation she can no longer have second-class citizens. Now, more than ever before, America is challenged to bring her noble dream into reality, and those who are working to implement the American dream are the true saviors of democracy.

Now may I suggest some of the things we must do if we are to make the American dream a reality. First I think all of us must develop a world perspective if we are to survive. The American dream will not become a reality devoid of the larger dream of a world of brotherhood and peace and good will. The world in which we live is a world of geographical oneness and we are challenged now to make it spiritually one ★

THE AUTHOR

Martin Luther King, Sr., was a preacher. There was no doubt that his son, Martin Luther King, Jr., would also become a preacher. After graduating from Morehouse College in 1948, he earned a divinity degree from Crozer Theological Seminary and a doctoral degree from Boston University. In 1954 he became pastor of the Dexter Avenue Baptist Church in Montgomery, Alabama. A year later, he was leading a boycott of the public bus system in Montgomery. His leadership ability and oratorical skills were evident. Within a few short years, he was recognized as the leader of the civil rights struggle in America. King was assassinated in Memphis, Tennessee, in 1968.

THE RESPONSE

In this speech to the students at Lincoln University, Dr. King's view of the challenge facing the United States is very clear. So is his feeling of how urgently the country needs to solve the problem of race. At the March on Washington, which took place in August 1963, thousands of Americans demonstrated their concern as well. It was during this march that Dr. King delivered his famous "I Have a Dream" speech.

erly known
roducts, made Redu
n, chemical cousins that
enfluramine half of the

From an Address Delivered at the
Hotel Theresa, New York City · DECEMBER 31, 1964

MALCOLM X

1925–1965

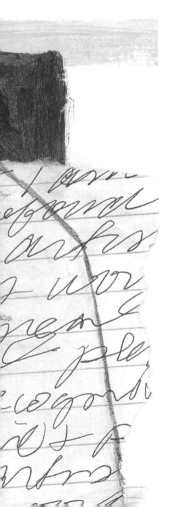

From the beginning, African Americans have had different views about how to fight slavery and racism in the United States. Some sought peaceful ways. They wanted to see the United States as an integrated society where all its citizens were treated equally. Others, however, felt armed rebellion was essential. They didn't believe African Americans could achieve their rights without a physical struggle. Some also felt that an integrated society should not be the goal, but rather that African Americans should take the opportunity for self-determination. Malcolm X was part of this militant, black nationalist tradition. His support of black self-help, self-determination, and self-defense appealed to many African Americans during the 1950s and 1960s. The following speech was delivered to thirty-seven black teenagers from McComb, Mississippi, who had come to New York for their Christmas vacation.

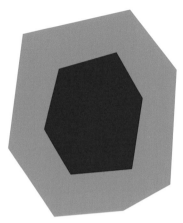ne of the first things I think young people, especially nowadays, should learn is how to see for yourself and listen for yourself and think for yourself. If you learn the habit of going by what you hear others say about someone, or going by what others think about someone, instead of searching that thing out for yourself and seeing for yourself, you will be walking west when you think you're going east, and you will be walking east when you think you're going west. This generation, especially of our people, has a burden, more so than any other time in history. The most important thing we can learn to do today is think for ourselves.

It's good to keep wide-open ears and listen to what everybody else has to say, but when you come to make decisions, you have to weigh all of what you've heard on its own, and place it where it belongs, and come to a decision for yourself; you'll never regret it. But if you form the habit of taking what someone else says about a thing without checking it out for yourself, you'll find that other people will have you hating your friends and loving your enemies. This is one of the things that our people are beginning to learn today—that it is very important to think out a situation for yourself. If you don't do it, you'll always be maneuvered into a situation where you are never fighting your actual enemies, where you will find yourself fighting your own self.

I think our people in this country are the best examples of that. Many of us want to be nonviolent and we talk very loudly, you know, about being nonviolent. Here in Harlem, where there are probably more black people concentrated than any place in the world, some talk that nonviolent talk too. But we find that they aren't nonviolent with each other. You can go out to Harlem Hospital, where there are more black patients than any hospital in the world, and see them going in there all cut up and shot up and busted up where they got violent with each other.

My experience has been that in many instances where you find Negroes talking about nonviolence, they are not nonviolent with each other, and they're not loving with each other, or forgiving with each other. Usually when they say they're nonviolent, they mean they're nonviolent with somebody else. I think you understand what I mean. They are nonviolent with the enemy. A person can come to your home, and if he's white and wants to heap some kind of brutality on you, you're nonviolent; or he can come to take your father and put a rope around his neck and you're nonviolent. But if another Negro just stomps his foot, you'll rumble him in a minute. Which shows you that there's an inconsistency there.

If the leaders of the nonviolent movement can go into

"WE ARE NOT FIGHTING FOR INTEGRATION, NOR ARE WE FIGHTING FOR SEPARATION. WE ARE FIGHTING FOR RECOGNITION AS HUMAN BEINGS."
—Malcolm X

the white community and teach nonviolence, good. I'd
go along with that. But as long as I see them teaching
nonviolence only in the black community, we can't go along
with that. We believe in equality, and equality means that
you have to put the same thing over here that you put over
there. And if black people alone are going to be the ones
who are nonviolent, then it's not fair. We throw ourselves
off guard. In fact, we disarm ourselves and make ourselves
defenseless. . . . ★

THE AUTHOR

Malcolm X was born in Omaha, Nebraska. Following a troubled childhood, he was sent to prison in 1946 when he was twenty-one years old. While in prison Malcolm embraced the Nation of Islam movement headed by Elijah Muhammad. Members of the Nation of Islam believed there should be a separate black country. After his release in 1952, Malcolm became a leading spokesman for the sect. Urban youth in particular responded to his fiery speeches. A rift developed between Malcolm and Elijah Muhammad in 1963, and Malcolm was suspended as a minister. After returning from a trip to Mecca in 1964, Malcolm established his own organization called the Organization of Afro-American Unity. He softened the separatist position he had accepted from the Black Muslims. On February 21, 1965, Malcolm was assassinated in New York.

THE RESPONSE

Two months after the speech to African-American students at the Theresa Hotel Malcolm X was killed in New York City. After his death, many people—African Americans and whites—began to look at Malcolm differently. They began to read his speeches and autobiography, *The Autobiography of Malcolm X*, written with Alex Haley. Because Malcolm had risen from the streets to a position of leadership, he was seen as a man of the people. And his advocacy of self-defense, self-determination, and self-reliance influenced the black power movement that was emerging at the time of his assassination.

A NEW DIRECTION

From a Speech Delivered at the University of California at Berkeley ★ NOVEMBER 16, 1966

STOKELEY CARMICHAEL
1941–2000

The civil rights movement that came of age in the 1950s was based on the principle of nonviolence. It included whites as well as African Americans. Almost all African-American leaders and organizations believed this approach was the best way to achieve equality and justice for all Americans. For some African Americans, however, the approach was too slow. For others, nonviolence was an inappropriate way to deal with the violence many African Americans faced daily. In 1966 a young, brash, and articulate Stokeley Carmichael introduced "black power." It became a symbol of a new, militant direction for many African Americans.

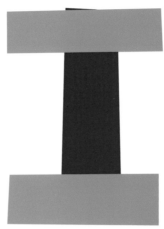t seems to me that the institutions that function in this country are clearly racist, and that they're built upon racism. And the question, then, is how can black people inside this country move? And then, how can white people, who say they're not a part of those institutions, begin to  move, and how then do we begin to clear away the obstacles that we have in this society that keep us from living like human beings. How can we begin to build institutions that will allow people to relate with each other as human beings? This country has never done that. Especially around the concept of white or black.

Now several people have been upset because we've said that integration was irrelevant when initiated by blacks and that in fact it was a subterfuge, an insidious subterfuge for the maintenance of white supremacy. We maintain that in the past six years or so this country has been feeding us a thalidomide drug of integration, and that some Negroes have been walking down a dream street talking about sitting next to white people, and that that does not begin to solve the problem. When we went to Mississippi, we did not go to sit next to Ross Barnett [former governor of Mississippi]; we did not go to sit next to Jim Clark [former sheriff of Dallas County, Selma, Alabama]; we went to get them out of our way, and people ought to understand that. We were never fighting for the right to integrate, we were fighting against white supremacy. . . .

Now we are engaged in a psychological struggle in this country and that struggle is whether or not black people have the right to use the words they want to use without white people giving their sanction to it. We maintain, whether they like it or not, we gon' use the words "black power" and let them address themselves to that. We are not gonna wait for white people to sanction black power. We're tired of waiting. Every time black people move in this country, they're forced to defend their position before they move. It's time that the people who're supposed to be defending their position do that. That's white people. They ought to start defending themselves, as to why they have oppressed and exploited us.

It is clear that when this country started to move in terms of slavery, the reason for a man being picked as a slave was one reason: because of the color of his skin. If one was black, one was automatically inferior, inhuman and therefore fit for slavery. So that the question of whether or not we are individually suppressed is nonsensical and is a downright lie. We are oppressed as a group because we are black, not because we are lazy, not because we're apathetic, not because we're stupid, not because we smell, not because we eat watermelon and have good rhythm. We are oppressed because we are black, and in order to get out of that oppression, one must feel the group power that one has.

"FOR RACISM TO DIE, A TOTALLY DIFFERENT AMERICA MUST BE BORN."
—Stokeley Carmichael

Not the individual power which this country then sets the criteria under which a man may come into it. That is what is called in this country as integration. You do what I tell you to do, and then we'll let you sit at the table with us. And then we are saying that we have to be opposed to that. We must now set a criterion, and that if there's going to be any integration it's going to be a two-way thing. If you believe in integration, you can come live in Watts. You can send your children to the ghetto schools. Let's talk about that. If you believe in integration, then we're going to start adopting us some white people to live in our neighborhood. So it is clear that the question is not one of integration or segregation. Integration is a man's ability to want to move in there by himself. If someone wants to live in a white neighborhood and he is black, that is his choice. It should be his right. It is not because white people will allow him. So, vice versa, if a black man wants to live in the slums, that should be his right. Black people will let him, that is the difference. ⭑

THE AUTHOR

After graduating from Howard University in 1961, Stokeley Carmichael joined the Student Non-Violent Coordinating Committee (SNCC) and became its chairman. Under Carmichael's leadership, SNCC helped to register many African Americans in the South to vote. The organization also participated in protest marches with other civil rights groups. Most SNCC members were college students. After leaving SNCC in 1967, Carmichael joined the Black Panthers, a militant group, and later moved to Guinea in Africa.

THE RESPONSE

One civil rights organization, the Congress of Racial Equality (CORE), said, "Black power is not black supremacy; it is a unified black voice reflecting racial pride in the tradition of our heterogeneous nation." Most traditional civil rights organizations, however, opposed the concept. But black power represented a shift in African-American communities, particularly among young people. Self-determination, black pride, and a recognition of an important African connection were at the center of this new movement.

"Hug [your] grandparents and say 'I want to thank you for what you've done to make me and my life possible.'"

—*Alex Haley*

From *Roots: The Saga of an American Family* ⋆ 1976

ALEX HALEY

1941–1992

With more emphasis on self-determination and the African connection came a greater interest in family heritage. Many African Americans wanted to know their family roots. But for most the task of tracing their history beyond slavery seemed almost impossible. Slaves were property and as such were often sold and resettled away from their families. Once sold, many siblings, and even husbands and wives, never saw one another again. But Alex Haley proved that with meticulous research, one's ancestry could be traced. His book *Roots* sparked national and international interest in genealogy.

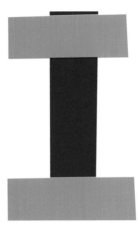t was a week after Kizzy's sixteenth birthday, the early morning of the first Monday of October, when the slave-row field hands were gathering as usual to leave for their day's work, when someone asked curiously, "Where Noah at?" Kunta, who happened to be standing nearby talking to Cato, knew immediately that he was gone. He saw heads glancing around, Kizzy's among them, straining to maintain a mask of casual surprise. Their eyes met—she had to look away.

"Thought he was out here early wid you," said Noah's mother Ada to Cato.

"Naw, I was aimin' to give 'im de debbil fo' sleepin' late," said Cato.

Cato went banging his fist at the closed door of the cabin, once occupied by the old gardener, but which Noah had inherited recently on his eighteenth birthday. Jerking the door open, Cato charged inside, shouting angrily, "Noah!" He came out looking worried. "Ain't like 'im," he said quietly. Then he ordered everyone to go quickly and search their cabins, the toilet, the storerooms, the fields.

All the others ran off in all directions; Kunta volunteered to search the barn. "NOAH! NOAH!" he called loudly for the benefit of any who might hear, although he knew there was no need of it, as the animals in their stalls stopped chewing their morning hay to look at him oddly. Then, peering from the door and seeing no one coming that way, Kunta hastened back inside to climb quickly to the hayloft, where he prostrated himself and made his second appeal to Allah for Noah's successful escape.

Cato worriedly dispatched the rest of the field hands off to their work, telling them that he and the fiddler would join them shortly; the fiddler had wisely volunteered to help with the fieldwork ever since his income from playing for dances had fallen off.

"B'lieve he done run," the fiddler muttered to Kunta as they stood in the backyard.

As Kunta grunted, Bell said, "He ain't never been missin', an' he don't slip off nights."

Then Cato said what was uppermost in all of their minds. "Gwine have to tell massa, Lawd have mercy!" After a hurried consultation, Bell recommended that Massa Waller not be told until after he had eaten his breakfast, "'case de boy done jes' eased off somewhere an' got scairt to slip back fo' it's dark again, less'n dem road paterollers cotches 'im."

Bell served the massa his favorite breakfast—canned peaches in heavy cream, hickory-smoked fried ham, scrambled eggs, grits, heated apple butter, and buttermilk biscuits—and waited for him to ask for his second cup of coffee before speaking.

"Massa—" she swallowed, "—Massa, Cato ax me to tell you

look like dat boy Noah ain't here dis mawnin'!"

The massa sat down his cup, frowning. "Where is he, then? Are you trying to tell me he's off drunk or tomcatting somewhere, and you think he'll slip back today, or are you saying you think he's trying to run?"

"All us sayin', Massa," Bell quavered, "is seem like he ain't here, an' us done searched eve'ywheres."

Massa Waller studied his coffee cup. "I'll give him until tonight—no, tomorrow morning—before I take action."

"Massa, he a good boy, born and bred right here on yo' place, an' work good all his life, ain't never give you or nobody a minute's trouble—"

He looked levelly at Bell. "If he's trying to run, he'll be sorry."

"Yassuh, Massa." Bell fled to the yard, where she told the others what the massa had said. But no sooner had Cato and the fiddler hurried off toward the fields than Massa Waller called Bell back and ordered the buggy ⋆

THE AUTHOR

Alex Haley was born in Ithaca, New York, and raised in Henning, Tennessee. After graduating from high school at the age of fifteen, he attended college for two years, then joined the United States Coast Guard. He began writing while in the Coast Guard. His career as a freelance writer began after he retired. In 1965 his first book, *The Autobiography of Malcolm X*, was published. It took him twelve years to research and write *Roots: The Saga of an American Family*. Haley published a number of other books, including *Roots: The Next Generation* and *Henning, Tennessee*.

THE RESPONSE

Roots: The Saga of an American Family was first excerpted in *Reader's Digest* in 1974 and received critical acclaim. The book was published in 1976. In January 1977, ABC-TV produced a twelve-hour series based on the book. It attracted more than 120 million viewers, a record number for television. *Roots* won numerous awards and was praised for its moving portrait of life under slavery. Because of *Roots*, many people, white and African-American, began to research their ancestry. Following the book's release, the United States Senate passed a resolution paying tribute to Alex Haley and comparing *Roots* to *Uncle Tom's Cabin* by Harriet Beecher Stowe. *Uncle Tom's Cabin*, published in 1852, helped many people see the horrors of slavery.

**From the Keynote Address,
National Democratic Convention, New York City** ★ 1976

BARBARA JORDAN

1936–1996

African Americans have struggled long to secure political equality. During slavery, only a few states allowed free African-American men to vote. Enslaved African Americans could not vote at all. Women, black and white, did not achieve the privilege of voting until the ratification of the Nineteenth Amendment in 1920.

Following the Civil War, the Fifteenth Amendment to the Constitution gave African-American men the right to vote. And they voted in large numbers. A significant number were elected to local and state offices in the South. By the 1900s, however, Jim Crow laws had stripped African Americans of most of their rights as citizens, including the right to vote. From the end of Reconstruction to the 1960s during the height of the civil rights movement, the majority of African Americans could not vote. The civil rights movement helped to restore many of these rights. Today, thousands of African Americans hold elected office across the country.

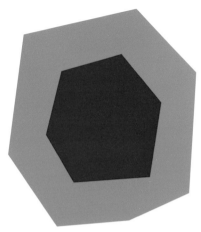

ne hundred and forty-four years ago, members of the Democratic Party met for the first time in convention to select their Presidential candidate. Since that time, Democrats have continued to convene once every four years to draft a party platform and nominate a Presidential candidate. Our meeting this week continues that tradition.

There is something different and special about this opening night. I am a keynote speaker.

In the intervening years since 1832, it would have been most unusual for any national political party to have asked a Barbara Jordan to make a keynote address . . . most unusual.

The past notwithstanding, a Barbara Jordan is before you tonight. This is one additional bit of evidence that the American Dream need not be deferred.

Now that I have this distinction, what should I say?

I could easily spend this time praising the accomplishments of this party and attacking the record of the Republicans.

I do not choose to do that.

I could list the many problems which cause people to feel cynical, frustrated, and angry: problems which include the lack of integrity in government; the feeling that the individual no longer counts; the realities of material and spiritual poverty; the feeling that the grand American experiment is failing . . . or has failed. Having described these and other problems, I could sit down without offering any solutions.

"WHAT THE PEOPLE WANT IS VERY SIMPLE. THEY WANT AN AMERICA AS GOOD AS ITS PROMISE."
—Barbara Jordan

I do not choose to do that either.

The citizens of America expect more. They deserve and want more than a recital of problems.

We are a people in a quandry about the present and in search of our future.

We are a people in search of a national community.

It is a search that is unending for we are not only trying to solve the problems of the moment—inflation, unemployment—but on a larger scale, we are attempting to fulfill the promise of America. We are attempting to fulfill our national purpose; to create and sustain a society in which all of us are equal ⋆

THE AUTHOR

In 1966 Barbara Jordan became the first African American elected to the Texas State Senate since 1883. In 1972 she was elected president pro tempore of the Texas Senate, becoming the first African-American woman in the country to preside over a legislative body. Jordan was elected to the United States House of Representatives in 1972, where she served until she retired in 1979.

Jordan was also one of the first African-American women to attend Boston University Law School (1956–1959).

THE RESPONSE

In 1974, as a member of the United States House of Representatives' Judiciary Committee, Barbara Jordan impressed the nation during the impeachment hearings of President Richard Nixon. A poised and eloquent speaker, she was viewed as a star on the rise in the Democratic Party. Her speech at the National Democratic Convention was thought to be the kind of spotlight she needed to pursue an even higher political office. Her retirement from politics in 1979, for health reasons, surprised many Democrats.

"Our flag is red,
white and blue, but
our nation is a rainbow
—red, yellow, brown,
black, and white—
we're all precious
in God's sight."

—Jesse Jackson

From an Address to the
National Democratic Convention ★ JULY 19, 1988

REVEREND JESSE JACKSON

1941–

In 1972 Eldridge Cleaver and Shirley Chisholm became the first African Americans to seek the office of president of the United States. Chisholm was the first African-American woman elected to the United States House of Representatives and Cleaver was a leader of the Black Panther organization and a successful writer. Neither garnered many votes. In 1984 Jesse Jackson mounted the first presidential campaign by an African American to win a significant number of votes, nearly three million. Using the experience he gained during the 1984 Democratic race, Jackson ran again in 1988. This time he won six million votes and had a major impact at the Democratic Convention.

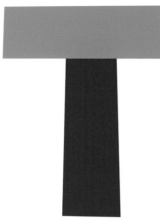onight, we pause and give praise and honor to God for being good enough to allow us to be at this place at this time. When I look out at this convention, I see the face of America, red, yellow, brown, black, and white. We are all precious in God's sight—the real rainbow coalition. All of us—all of us who are here think that we are seated. But we're really standing on someone's shoulders. Ladies and gentlemen, Mrs. Rosa Parks. The mother of the civil rights movement . . .

My right and my privilege to stand here before you has been won—won in my lifetime—by the blood and the sweat of the innocent . . . Dr. Martin Luther King, Jr., lies only a few miles from us tonight. Tonight he must feel good as he looks down upon us. We sit here together, a rainbow coalition—the sons and daughters of slavemasters and the sons and daughters of slaves sitting together around a common table, to decide the direction of our party and our country. His heart would be full tonight.

As a testament to the struggles of those who have gone before; as a legacy for those who will come after; as a tribute to the endurance, the patience, the courage of our forefathers and mothers; as an assurance that their prayers are being answered, their work has not been in vain, and hope is eternal, tomorrow night my name will go into nomination for the presidency of the United States of America.

We meet tonight at the crossroads, a point of decision. Shall we expand, be inclusive, find unity and power; or suffer division and impotence.

We're come to Atlanta, the cradle of the old South, the crucible of the new South.

Tonight there is a sense of celebration because we are moved, fundamentally moved from racial battlegrounds by law, to economic common ground, with the moral challenge to move to higher ground; common ground! . . . Common ground! That's the challenge of our party tonight.

Left wing. Right wing. Progress will not come through boundless liberalism nor static conservatism, but at the critical mass of mutual survival.

When we divide, we cannot win. We must find common ground as a basis for survival. The day when we debated, differed, deliberated, agreed to agree, agree to disagree, when we had the good judgment to argue a case and then not self-destruct, George Bush was just a little further away from the White House and a little closer to private life.

Tonight I salute Governor Michael Dukakis. He has run—He has run a well-managed and dignified campaign.

No matter how tired or how tried, he always resisted the

temptation to stoop to demagoguery. I have watched a good mind fast at work, with steel nerves guiding his campaign out of the crowded field without appeal to the worst in us.

I have watched his perspective grow as his environment has expanded. I've seen his toughness and tenacity close up, knew his commitment to public service. . . .

His foreparents came to America on immigrant ships. My foreparents came to America on slave ships. But whatever the original ships, we are in the same boat tonight. . . .

Our choice? Full participation in a Democratic government or more abandonment and neglect. And so this night, we choose not a false sense of independence not our capacity to survive and endure. Tonight we choose interdependency, and our capacity to act and unite for the greater good ★

THE AUTHOR

Reverend Jesse Jackson's involvement in
the civil rights movement began when, as
a student at North Carolina Agriculture
and Technical College in Greensboro, he
helped to integrate public facilities there.
In 1963 he joined the Southern Christian
Leadership Conference (SCLC) and helped
rally ministers in Chicago behind Dr. Martin
Luther King, Jr., and SCLC. His speaking
and organizational ability helped him rise
to a leadership position in SCLC. Jackson
was with Dr. King when the leader was
assassinated in 1968. In 1971 Jackson formed
his own organization, Operation Push, in
Chicago, following a dispute with other SCLC
leaders. He became African Americans' most
vocal leader.

THE RESPONSE

Jesse Jackson had attempted to win the
Democratic nomination for president in 1984.
Although he mounted a spirited campaign,
many people did not consider his efforts a
serious challenge for the nomination. The
year 1988, however, was different. Jackson
used the experience he had gained in 1984
to conduct a well-managed campaign that
made him the first African American to
seriously make a bid for the presidential
nomination of a major political party.
Jackson received 82 percent of the
African-American vote and 20 percent
of the white vote during the Democratic
primaries. Jackson continues to speak
out on issues concerning African
Americans and the poor.

From a Speech Delivered at the Congressional Black Caucus
Conference, Washington, D.C. • **NOVEMBER 26, 1987**

MARIAN WRIGHT EDELMAN

1939–

African Americans have been in the forefront of their struggle for equality and justice. They have, however, provided leadership for many other causes and issues as well. A few of those issues include women's rights, children's rights, world hunger, and the anti-apartheid movement in South Africa.

A. Phillip Randolph was an important labor leader as well as a civil rights leader. The colorful attorney Florence Kennedy was a leader in the women's movement. Randall Robinson helped make apartheid an important issue in the United States, leading to the end of that horrible system.

Marian Wright Edelman has been a leading voice for issues relating to young people in this country and around the world. She has lobbied Congress to enact laws, and has marshaled organizations and businesses to help care for and protect children.

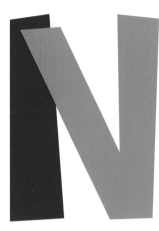ot only are too many black babies and youths fighting poverty and sickness and homelessness and too little early childhood stimulation and weak basic skills preparation, they are fighting AIDS and other sexually transmitted diseases; drug, tobacco, and alcohol addiction, and crime, which hopelessness and the absence of constructive alternatives and support systems in their lives leave them prey to. A black baby is seven or eight times more likely to be an AIDS victim than a white baby, and minority teens (fifteen to nineteen) are the highest risk group for a range of sexually transmitted diseases. A black youth is five times more likely than a white youth to end up in an institution and is nearly as likely to be in prison as he is to be in college. Between 1979 and 1985 the number of black youth in juvenile detention facilities rose by 40 percent while the number of black youth entering college immediately after high school graduation fell by 4 percent. More black males go to prison each year than go to college. There are more black drug addicts than there are black doctors or lawyers.

Now some of you sitting here will ask what this has to do with you. You struggled and beat the odds and those folks who haven't made it could do the same. Others of you will rightfully say you're already doing your bit for the race by achieving yourself and by contributing to black organizations. Still others place the blame for growing black family poverty and weakening community bonds and support systems on urbanization and the continuing racial discrimination in national life which devalues black talent and curbs black opportunity.

As many nuggets of truth as each of these views may contain, I will simply say that unless the black middle class begins to exert more effective and sustained leadership with and without the black community on behalf of black children and families both as personal role models and value instillers and as persistent advocates for national, state, and local policies—funded policies—that assure our children the health and child care, education, housing, and jobs they need to grow into self-sufficient adults, to form healthy families, and to carry on the black tradition of achievement, then all of our Mercedeses and Halston frocks will not hide our essential failure as a generation of black haves who did not protect the black future during our watch.

Just as our nation is committing moral and economic suicide by permitting one in four of its preschool children to be poor, one in five to be at risk of being a teen parent, one in six to have no health insurance, and one in seven to face dropping out of school at a time when the pool of available young people to support an aging population and form a strong workforce is shrinking, so we are committing racial suicide by not sounding the alarm and protecting our own children from the poverty that ravages their dreams. For America will not treat our children fairly unless we make it.

We must recapture and care about our lost children and help them gain the confidence, self-esteem, values, and real-world opportunities—education, jobs, and higher education which they need to be strong future guardians of the black community's heritage ★

THE AUTHOR

Marian Wright Edelman was born and raised in Bennettsville, South Carolina. After graduating from Spelman College and Yale Law School, she worked for the NAACP Legal Defense and Educational Fund as a staff attorney. In 1964 she established an NAACP Legal Defense and Educational Fund office in Jackson, Mississippi. In 1968 she founded the Washington Research Project of the Southern Center for Public Policy. The project developed into the Children's Defense Fund, one of the leading children's advocacy agencies.

THE RESPONSE

Edelman's speech to the Congressional Black Caucus, a group that includes African-American United States Representatives, coincided with the release of her book *Families in Peril: An Agenda for Social Change.* The book presented Edelman's views on the problems facing families and children, as well as some solutions she believes are possible.

Marian Wright Edelman has become one of the most effective lobbyists for child welfare issues. Under her direction, the Children's Defense Fund has tackled issues such as teenage pregnancy, inadequate health care, violence against children, and lack of quality education.

PARADISE

BELOVED

TAR BABY

From the Nobel Lecture in Literature,
Delivered In Stockholm, Sweden ★ DECEMBER 7, 1993

TONI 1931– MORRISON

For years, African-American writers found it difficult to get published. The Harlem Renaissance of the 1920s and 1930s created new opportunities. Some writers, mostly African-American males, were able to join the ranks of America's writers. But by the late 1930s, those chances had faded for most aspiring African-American writers. The 1950s and 1960s, spurred by the civil rights movement, saw an increased interest in African-American literature. Some African-American male writers were published during this period, but very few African-American women. James Baldwin, Eldridge Cleaver, Leroi Jones, Ernest J. Gaines, Julius Lester, John Edgar Wideman, and Claude Brown are a few of the African-American males to achieve literary success during this period.

During the 1990s and the first decade of the twenty-first century, many African-American women writers have achieved literary success. They owe their opportunities to the groundbreaking achievements of writers such as Alice Walker, Maya Angelou, and Toni Morrison. The works produced by these women in the 1970s and 1980s paved the way for this new group of women writers.

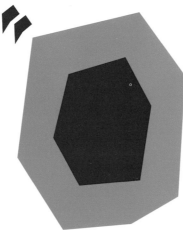

"nce upon a time there was an old woman. Blind but wise." Or was it an old man? A guru, perhaps. Or a griot soothing restless children. I have heard this story, or one exactly like it, in the lore of several cultures. "Once upon a time there was an old woman. Blind. Wise."

In the version I know the woman is the daughter of slaves, black American, and lives alone in a small house outside of town. Her reputation for wisdom is without peer and without question. Among her people she is both the law and its transgression. The honor she is paid and the awe in which she is held reach beyond her neighborhood to places far away; to the city where the intelligence of rural prophets is the source of much amusement.

One day the woman is visited by some young people who seem to be bent on disproving her clairvoyance and showing her up for the fraud they believe she is. Their plan is simple: They enter her house and ask the one question the answer to which rides solely on her difference from them, a difference they regard as a profound liability: her blindness. They stand before her, and one of them says, "Old woman, I hold in my hand a bird. Tell me whether it is living or dead."

She does not answer, and the question is repeated. "Is the bird I am holding living or dead?"

Still she doesn't answer. She is blind and cannot see her visitors, let alone what is in their hands. She does not know their color, gender, or homeland. She only knows their motive.

"OUR ANCESTORS ARE AN EVER WIDENING CIRCLE OF HOPE."
—Toni Morrison

The old woman's silence is so long, the young people have trouble holding their laughter.

Finally she speaks and her voice is soft but stern. "I don't know," she says. "I don't know whether the bird you are holding is dead or alive, but what I do know is that it is in your hands. It is in your hands."

Her answer can be taken to mean: If it is dead, you have either found it that way or you have killed it. If it is alive, you can still kill it. Whether it is to stay alive, it is your decision. Whatever the case, it is your responsibility.

For parading their power and her helplessness, the young visitors are reprimanded, told they are responsible not only for the act of mockery but also for the small bundle of life sacrificed to achieve its aims. The blind woman shifts attention away from assertions of power to the instrument through which that power is exercised ⋆

THE AUTHOR

Toni Morrison was born in Lorain, Ohio. She graduated from Howard University and received her master's degree from Cornell University. Morrison has held teaching posts at Yale, Bard, Rutgers University, Howard University, and Texas Southern University. While she was a senior editor at Random House, she launched her writing career. Her first book, *The Bluest Eye,* was published in 1970. She has published nine other books.

THE RESPONSE

Toni Morrison's body of work has ensured her a place among the giants of world literature. She won a National Book Critics Award in 1977 for *Song of Solomon* and a Pulitzer Prize in 1988 for *Beloved.* In 2000 she was presented a National Humanities Medal by President Bill Clinton for her contributions to American cultural life and thought. In 1993 she became the first African-American woman and the first woman since 1938 to receive the prestigious Nobel Prize in literature.

"The Miseducation of Lauryn Hill" ★ 1998

LAURYN HILL

1975–

In the 1970s a new music form began that would eventually change popular music around the world. It was called rap. Like most new music forms, rap was at first an underground phenomenon. It could be heard mostly at clubs in urban areas. But by the 1980s, rap music had gained national exposure. Rap artists such as Run DMC, Kurtis Blow, and Grand Master Flash became big stars.

As rap music grew, other art forms such as break dancing and graffiti art became associated with it. Rappers and their supporters dressed differently, too. A new subculture called hip-hop was born. Hip-hop is now an important part of American culture. By the end of the twentieth century, Lauren Hill had emerged as one of the leading stars of hip-hop music.

y world, it moves so fast today.

The past it seems so far away

and life squeezes so tight that I can't breathe.

And every time I've tried to be

what someone else thought of me;

so caught up, I was unable to achieve.

But deep in my heart,

the answer it was in me.

And I made up my mind

to define my own destiny.

My own destiny

And deep in my heart

And deep in my heart,

the answer it was in me.

And I made up my mind

to define my own destiny.

I look at my environment

and wonder where the fire went.

What happened to ev'rything we used to be?

I hear so many cry for help,
searching outside themselves.
Now I know that His strength is within me.
And deep in my heart,
the answer it was in me.
And I made up my mind
to define my own destiny.

My own destiny
And deep in my heart
And deep in my heart,
the answer it was in me.
And I made up my mind
to define my own destiny ★

THE AUTHOR

Lauryn Hill wanted to pursue a career in entertainment. The South Orange, New Jersey, native, however, followed her parents' wishes to get an education and entered Columbia University. She had already formed a rap group called the Fugees with friends Wyclef Jean and Prakazrel (Pras) Michel. During her freshman year at Columbia, the Fugees released its first album with moderate success. Their second album, *The Score*, sold seventeen million copies and established the Fugees as a top act in the record industry.

THE RESPONSE

In 1998 Hill released her solo album *The Miseducation of Lauryn Hill*. It was based on Hill's experiences, and dealt with topics such as prejudice and materialism. It was seen as a breakthrough record that led other rap stars to record songs that addressed meaningful topics. Hill won five Grammy awards in 1998 for her work, giving her national and international recognition.

CONCLUSION

The African-American journey in the United States has not been an easy one. For almost 250 years, the majority of African Americans were held in bondage. Soon after slavery came to an end, a new system called segregation took its place. Both were designed to strip African Americans of their human dignity, their rights as citizens, and their freedom. In spite of seemingly impossible obstacles imposed upon them by these systems, African Americans forged ahead with determination and hope. While doing so, they made enormous contributions to our country and to the world.

It is totally impossible to understand the history of the United States without considering the crucial role played by African Americans. From the beginning, they have been central to our country's growth and development. For centuries, they provided a source of free labor in this country. They have come to our country's defense in times of war. They have made significant discoveries and have created important inventions. They have made enormous contributions in art, music, science, politics, and medicine. There is no way our country could be what it is today without African Americans.

Powerful Words is intended to give the reader a better understanding of the African-American journey in the United States by using words from African Americans themselves. There are so many powerful voices. I urge readers to seek out those voices and learn more about our country.

AUTHOR'S NOTE

I realized the power words had to influence and motivate people at an early age. As a small kid growing up in Mansfield, Louisiana, I was often mesmerized by the persuasive power possessed by the pastor of the church my family attended. Reverend M. B. Collins had a way of using words to make the stories and the characters in the Bible come alive. He could make his congregation connect to those characters and stories in very personal ways. In fact, I could close my eyes during his sermons and visualize myself as David, Joshua, or Moses. For a while, I wanted to be a minister just like Reverend Collins.

My mother was someone who also impressed me during those years. She had the ability to use words to get her children to do what she wanted. When forceful words were needed, she used them. When words that made us feel guilty about a bad deed we had done were necessary, they flowed easily from her mouth. She could even elicit sympathy for herself with the right words and accompanying expression.

In essence, I have always been impressed by the power of words. That's probably the primary reason why I chose to become a writer.

Several years ago, while listening to a tape of Dr. Martin Luther King, Jr.'s "I Have a Dream" speech, I thought about the enormous impact his words had at the March on Washington in 1963 and still have on our society today. Most people in America and many around the world are familiar with this great speech. But other African Americans have made important speeches, too. Many have used the written word to help shape and change our nation and our world. But not too many people know who most of these African Americans are, nor are they familiar with their contributions.

Powerful Words provides an opportunity for young readers to learn about some of the African Americans who have used the power of words to help change our nation. I am sure *Powerful Words* would make my former pastor, Reverend Collins, proud if he were still alive. And I am sure he would have the appropriate words to describe the book's importance.

Wade Hudson

CHRONOLOGY

1500s — The British, Dutch, Spanish, and Portuguese begin trafficking African people in the brutal slave trade.

1600 — Queen Nzingha of Angola fights against the Portuguese and the enslavement of her people.

1619 — The first boatload of Africans arrives in Virginia.

1660 — The number of American slaves increases rapidly as the British gain control over much of the slave trade.

1700

1770 — Phillis Wheatley publishes her first poem, becoming the earliest-known published African-American woman writer.

The American Revolution begins. The thirteen American colonies fight for their independence from British rule. One of the first casualties of the war is a black man, Crispus Attucks.

1776 — The Declaration of Independence is signed, making the thirteen colonies an independent nation.

1780 — The first official mutual aid society, the African Union Society of Newport, Rhode Island, is formed.

1787 — The African Free School, the first free secular school in New York City, opens.

The Free African Society of Philadelphia, organized by Richard Allen and Absalom Jones, is formed.

The African Grand Lodge is established by Prince Hall.

1791 — Benjamin Banneker becomes the first African American to publish an almanac. He sends a letter to Secretary of State Thomas Jefferson, urging the future president to address the slavery problem.

Toussaint L'Ouverture leads a successful slave revolt in Haiti. Haiti becomes the first independent black nation in the Western Hemisphere.

1793 — The Fugitive Slave Act is passed. This law makes harboring an escaped slave a criminal act.

1798	James Forten, Sr., establishes a successful sail-making shop in Philadelphia.
1806	The African Meeting House in Boston, Massachusetts, is the first major building in Boston constructed solely by African Americans.
1807	Britain outlaws the slave trade.
1808	The United States bars importation of new slaves into U.S. territory (largely ignored).
1821	The first black theatrical company, the African Grove Theatre, is formed in New York City.
1822	Denmark Vesey organizes a slave revolt in Charleston, South Carolina.
1827	*Freedom's Journal,* the first black newspaper in America, with John Russwurm and Samuel Cornish serving as its editors, is published.
1829	*David Walker's Appeal* is published.
1831	Nat Turner leads a slave rebellion in Southampton, Virginia.
1833	Britain abolishes slavery in the British Empire.
1839	Joseph Cinque and other captured Africans take over the slave ship *Amistad,* demanding to be returned to Africa. They are ultimately set free by a United States Supreme Court decision in 1841.
1843	Sojourner Truth starts her own campaign against slavery.
	Norbert Rillieux patents his vacuum evaporation system, which revolutionizes the sugar industry and food production in general.
1848	The right of women to vote is proposed for the first time by women's rights leaders Elizabeth Cady Stanton and Lucretia Mott.
1849	Harriet Tubman escapes slavery and begins conducting on the Underground Railroad.
1850	The Underground Railroad is fully functioning, helping Southern slaves escape to the North and to Canada.
1851	Sojourner Truth addresses the Ohio Women's Rights Convention.

1852	Frederick Douglass delivers a speech to the Rochester Antislavery Sewing Society.
1853	William Wells Brown becomes America's first African-American novelist when his book *Clotel; Or, the President's Daughter: A Narrative of Slave Life in the United States* is published in England.
1854	Frances Ellen Watkins Harper publishes the collection of poetry that launched her career, entitled *Poems on Miscellaneous Subjects.* Her first volume of poetry was published in 1851.
1855	John Mercer Langston becomes the first African-American elected to office in the United States when he becomes clerk of Brownhelm Township in Lorraine, Ohio.
1856	After being taken from Mississippi to California by her master, Biddy Mason gains her freedom. She becomes a wealthy landowner and one of the first black women in California to own property.
1857	The Dred Scott decision is rendered by the United States Supreme Court.
1861	The Civil War begins between the North and the South.
1863	President Abraham Lincoln signs the Emancipation Proclamation, granting freedom to slaves in the states that are at war against the Union.
1864	Rebecca Lee is the first African-American woman in the United States to receive a medical degree.
1865	The Civil War ends with a Union victory.
	Henry Highland Garnet delivers a speech in the hall of the United States House of Representatives.
	The Thirteenth Amendment abolishes slavery.
1868	The Fourteenth Amendment provides African-Americans protection and privileges of natural citizens and gives them Constitutional guarantees.
	John Mercer Langston founds and organizes the law department at Howard University.

1870	Hiram M. Revels becomes the first African-American United States senator when he is elected from the state of Mississippi.
	The Fifteenth Amendment guarantees the right to vote to all men.
1872	Charlotte Ray becomes the first African-American woman to receive a law degree in the United States.
	P.B.S. Pinchback of Louisiana becomes the first African American to serve as governor of a state.
1876	Blanche K. Bruce delivers a speech to the United States Senate.
	Meharry Medical College becomes the first medical school founded for the education of African Americans.
1877	Henry Ossian Flipper becomes the first African American to graduate from the United States Military Academy.
1878	Benjamin "Pap" Singleton solicits southern blacks to migrate to the West.
1882	Lewis H. Latimer patents the first cost-efficient method of producing carbon filaments for electric lights.
1883	Jan Matzeliger patents the first successful shoe lasting machine.
1892	Ida B. Wells starts her crusade against the lynching of African Americans. She later helps to found the National Association for the Advancement of Colored People (NAACP).
1893	Dr. Daniel Hale Williams becomes the first person to perform a heart operation successfully.
1895	Booker T. Washington delivers his Atlanta Compromise speech at the Atlanta Exposition.
	Ida B. Wells Barnett publishes *The Red Record*, a pamphlet that exposes lynching in America.
1896	Mary Church Terrell is elected president of the National Association of Colored Women.
	In *Plessy* v. *Ferguson*, the United States Supreme Court upholds legal segregation.

1900

1897	Andrew J. Beard patents a coupling device for railroad cars.
1898	Mary Church Terrell delivers a speech to the National American Suffrage Association in Washington, D.C.
1899	Mary Eliza Mahoney is the first African-American woman to graduate from a professional white nursing school.
1900	James Weldon and J. Rosamond Johnson write "Lift Ev'ry Voice and Sing," the black national anthem.
1903	*The Souls of Black Folks,* by W.E.B. DuBois, is published.
	Maggie Lena Walker establishes the St. Luke Penny Savings Bank, which becomes the St. Luke Bank and Trust Company. She becomes America's first black woman bank president.
1904	Mary McLeod Bethune establishes a school now known as Bethune-Cookman University.
1908	Jack Johnson becomes the first African-American heavyweight champion when he knocks out Tommy Burns in fourteen rounds.
1910	The National Association for the Advancement of Colored People (NAACP) is formally established.
	Madame C. J. Walker opens her own beautycare factory. She becomes America's first black millionaire.
1914	The Universal Negro Improvement Association (UNIA) is formed by Marcus Garvey.
	World War I begins. The United States enters in 1917.
1915	The great migration of African Americans from the rural South to northern industrial cities is well underway.
	Birth of a Nation, a blatantly racist film, is released to a storm of protest in African-American communities.
1920s	The Nineteenth Amendment to the U.S. Constitution guarantees women the right to vote.
	The Harlem Renaissance is at its height.

1921	Langston Hughes pens his famous poem, "The Negro Speaks of Rivers."
1922	Bessie Coleman, the first African-American female pilot, performs an air show in Chicago.
1923	Garrett A. Morgan patents a three-way automatic traffic signal.
1926	Negro History Week is begun by Carter G. Woodson. It is now Black History Month.
1929	The Great Depression begins.
1935	The National Council of Negro Women is formed.
1936	Jesse Owens becomes the first athlete to win four gold medals in a single Olympics.
1937	*Their Eyes Were Watching God,* a novel by Zora Neale Hurston, is published.
1938	Thomas A. Dorsey's popular gospel song, "Take My Hand, Precious Lord" is published.
1939	World War II begins.
1940	*Native Son,* a novel by Richard Wright, is published.
	Frederick McKinley Jones patents a practical refrigeration system for trucks and railroad cars.
	Dr. Charles Richard Drew is the first person to set up a blood bank.
1941	*Who, The Magazine about People*, vol.1, 1, publishes an article entitled "Faith that Moved a Dump Heap," written by Mary McLeod Bethune.
	The United States enters World War II.
1945	World War II ends.
1946	Paul Robeson delivers a speech at the Conference for Equal Rights for Negroes in the Arts, Sciences and Professions.
1947	Jackie Robinson becomes the first African American to play Major League baseball in the modern era when he joins the Brooklyn Dodgers.

1948	Alice Coachman becomes the first African-American woman to win a gold medal in the Olympic Games.
1950	Gwendolyn Brooks becomes the first African American to win a Pulitzer Prize in literature.
	Ralph Bunche is the first African American to win the Nobel Peace Prize.
	Earl Lloyd becomes the first African American to play in the National Basketball Association when he suits up for the Washington Capitols. Charles Cooper is the first to be drafted by an NBA team, the Boston Celtics.
1954	The United States Supreme Court rules in *Brown* v. *Board of Education of Topeka, Kansas,* that segregation is unconstitutional.
1955	Rosa Parks refuses to give her seat to a white man on a Montgomery, Alabama, bus. Her refusal sparks a boycott headed by Dr. Martin Luther King, Jr.
1957	Althea Gibson becomes the first African American to win a Wimbledon singles tennis title.
1959	Lorraine Hansberry's play *A Raisin in the Sun* wins the New York Drama Critics Award.
1960	Wilma Rudolph becomes the first woman to win three gold medals in track in a single Olympics.
1961	Dr. Martin Luther King, Jr., delivers a speech at Lincoln University in Pennsylvania.
	The Freedom Rides begin.
1962	South African leader Nelson Mandela is imprisoned.
1963	A Birmingham, Alabama, church is bombed, killing four black children.
	The March on Washington is held.
1964	Malcolm X delivers a speech at the Hotel Theresa.
	The Civil Rights Act is passed.

1965	Malcolm X is assassinated.
	The Voting Rights Bill is passed, ending literacy tests for voters.
1966	Stokeley Carmichael delivers a speech at the University of California at Berkeley.
1968	Dr. Martin Luther King, Jr., is assassinated.
	Arthur Ashe becomes the first African-American male to win a major tennis tournament when he captures the singles title at the United States Lawn Tennis Association Open Tournament.
1976	*Roots,* a novel by Alex Haley, is published.
	Barbara Jordan delivers the keynote address at the National Democratic Convention.
1983	Guion Bluford, Jr., becomes the first African American to make a space flight.
	January 20 is declared a federal holiday in honor of Dr. Martin Luther King, Jr.
1987	Marian Wright Edelman delivers a speech at the Congressional Black Caucus Conference.
1988	Jesse Jackson becomes the first African American to mount a serious run for the presidency of the United States; he delivers a speech at the National Democratic Convention.
1990	Nelson Mandela is released from prison.
1992	Mae C. Jemison becomes the first African-American woman to make a space flight.
1993	Toni Morrison becomes the first African American to win the Nobel Prize in literature.
1998	Randall Robinson's *Defending the Spirit: A Black Life in America* is published.
	Lauryn Hill's solo album *The Miseducation of Lauryn Hill* is released.
2000	
2001	Colin L. Powell becomes secretary of state under George W. Bush.

SOURCES

The text excerpts included in this book come from a variety of sources.

Boyd, Herb, ed. *Autobiography of a People: Three Centuries of African American History Told by Those Who Lived It*. New York: Anchor Books, 2000.

> Richard Allen, pp. 41–3.

Carver, George Washington. Go to http://www.gardenforum.com. Click on Cornucopia, then click on Plants & People. Next choose George Washington Carver, then pick Carver's Spirituality and go to the end of the selection.

Dorsey, Thomas A. "Take My Hand, Precious Lord." Copyright © 1938 by Hill and Range Songs, Inc. Copyright renewed, assigned to Uni-Chappell Music, Inc., New York, New York. Belinda Music, Publisher.

DuBois, W. E. B. *The Souls of Black Folk*. Avenel, New Jersey: Gramercy Books, 1903, pp. 33–46.

Foner, Philip, ed. *The Voice of Black America: Major Speeches by Negroes in the United States, 1797–1971*. New York: Simon & Schuster, 1972.

> Frederick Douglass, pp. 105–29.
> Marcus Garvey, pp. 749–57.
> Paul Robeson, pp. 833–36.
> Martin Luther King, Jr., pp. 933–43.
> Malcolm X, pp. 1005–10.
> Stokeley Carmichael, pp. 1034–40.

Gates, Jr., Henry Louis, ed. *The Norton Anthology of African American Literature*. New York: Norton, 1997.

> Langston Hughes, p. 1254.

Haley, Alex. *Roots*. Garden City, New York: Doubleday, 1976, chap. 83.

Halliburton, Warren J., ed. *Historic Speeches of African Americans*. New York: Franklin Watts, 1993.

> Barbara Jordan, pp. 161–66.

Hill, Lauryn. "The Miseducation of Lauryn Hill." Copyright ©1998 Sony/ATV Tunes LLC, Obverse Creation Music and Jermaine Music. All rights administered by Sony/ATV Music Publishing, 8 Music Square West, Nashville, TN 37203.

Hurston, Zora Neale. *Their Eyes Were Watching God*. New York: Perennial Classics, 1937, chap. 20.

Lerner, Gerda, ed. *Black Women in White America: A Documentary History*. New York: Vintage Books, 1972.

  Mary McLeod Bethune, pp. 135–43.

Mullane, Deirdre, ed.. *Crossing the Danger Water*. New York: Anchor Books, 1993.

  Benjamin Banneker, pp. 48–50.
  Samuel Cornish and John Russwurm, pp. 63–66.
  David Walker, pp. 76–85.
  Dred Scott, pp. 134–35.
  Sojourner Truth, p. 186.
  Frances Ellen Watkins Harper, p. 202.
  Henry Highland Garnet, pp. 223–33.
  Blanche K. Bruce, pp. 312–13.
  Ida B. Wells Barnett, pp. 395–401.
  James Weldon Johnson and J. Rosamond Johnson, p. 443.
  Thurgood Marshall, pp. 622–25.

Parks, Rosa, and James Haskins. *My Story*. New York: Penguin, 1992, pages 113–16.

Ploski, Harry A. and James Williams, eds. *The Negro Almanac, A Reference Work on the African American*. Fifth edition. Detroit, MI: Gale Research, 1989.

  Booker T. Washington, pp. 148–149.
  Jesse Jackson, pp. 180–182.

Straub, Deborah Gillan, ed. *Voices of Multicultural America: Notable Speeches Delivered by African, Asian, Hispanic and Native Americans, 1790–1995*. Farmington Hills, MI: Gale Research, 1996.

  Marian Wright Edelman, pp. 342–46.
  Toni Morrison, pp. 892–96.

Terrell, Mary Church. Go to http://memory.loc.gov. Select Collection Finder, then click on List All Collections. Scroll down to African Americans—Daniel A. P. Murray—Pamphlets—1818–1907. Choose Browse Author Index, and select From Moreau to Tillman. Scroll down and click on Mary Church Terrell.

Wright, Richard. *Native Son*. New York: Perennial Classics, 1940, Book One: Fear.

The short quotes scattered throughout this book come from two sources.

Riley, Dorothy Winbush, ed. *My Soul Looks Back, 'Less I Forget: A Collection of Quotations by People of Color*. New York: HarperCollins, 1991.

> Allen, Richard, p. 130.
> Banneker, Benjamin, p. 63.
> Barnett, Ida B. Wells, p. 415.
> Bethune, Mary McLeod, p. 338.
> Carver, George Washington, p. 111.
> Douglass, Frederick, p. 175.
> DuBois, W. E. B., p. 246.
> Garnet, Henry Highland, p. 405.
> Garvey, Marcus, p. 18.
> Harper, Frances Ellen Watkins, p. 452.
> Hughes, Langton, p. 293.
> Hurston, Zora Neale, p. 237.
> Johnson, James Weldon, p. 92.
> King, Jr., Martin Luther, p. 89.
> Parks, Rosa, p. 97.
> Robeson, Paul, p. 149.
> Russwurm, John, p. 46.
> Terrell, Mary Church, p. 255.
> Truth, Sojourner, p. 338.
> Washington, Booker T., p. 69.
> Wright, Richard, p. 176.

Stenn, J. A., comp. and ed. *Quotations for Kids*. Brookfield, Connecticut: The Millbrook Press, 1991.

> Carmichael, Stokeley, p. 153.
> Haley, Alex, p. 95.
> Jackson, Jesse, p. 61.
> Jordan, Barbara, p. 18.
> Malcolm X, p. 45.
> Marshall, Thurgood, p. 71.

INDEX

CREDITS

From "Faith that Moved a Dump Heap" by Mary McLeod Bethune. Published in *Who, The Magazine about People*, vol.1.1, 3 (June 1941), pgs. 31-34. Copyright © 1941.

From *Their Eyes Were Watching God* by Zora Neale Hurston. Copyright © 1937 by Harper & Row Publishers Inc; copyright renewed 1965 by John C. Hurston and Joel Hurston. Reprinted by permission of HarperCollins Publishers, Inc.

"Take My Hand, Precious Lord" by Thomas A. Dorsey. Copyright © 1938 by Hill and Range Songs, Inc. Copyright renewed. Copyright Uni-Chappell Music, Inc. Used by permission of Warner Bros.

From *Native Son* by Richard Wright. Copyright © 1940 by Richard Wright; copyright renewed 1968 by Ellen Wright. Reprinted by permission of HarperCollins Publishers, Inc.

From *Rosa Parks: My Story* by Rosa Parks with Jim Haskins. Copyright © 1992 by Rosa Parks. Used by permission of Penguin Putnam, Inc.

From "The American Dream" by Martin Luther King, Jr. Copyright © 1961 by Martin Luther King, Jr.; copyright renewed. Used by permission.

From "To Young People" by Malcolm X. Copyright © 1964 by Malcolm X. Copyright © 1992. Used by permission.

From "Black Power" by Stokley Carmichael. Copyright © 1966 by Stokely Carmichael; copyright renewed 1994. Used by permission.

From *Roots: The Saga of an American Family* by Alex Haley. Copyright © 1974, 1976 by Alex Haley; copyright © 2002. Used by permission of Bantam Doubleday Dell.